Instructor
Excellence

Bob Powers

Foreword by
Malcolm S. Knowles

Instructor Excellence

MASTERING
THE DELIVERY
OF TRAINING

Jossey-Bass Publishers · San Francisco

For international orders, please contact your local Paramount Publishing International office.

TCF Manufactured in the United States of America on Lyons Falls Pathfinder Tradebook. This paper is acid-free and 100 percent totally chlorine-free.

Library of Congress Cataloging-in-Publication Data

Powers, Bob, [date]
    Instructor excellence : mastering the delivery of training / Bob Powers.
        p.   cm. — (The Jossey-Bass management series)
    Includes bibliographical references and index.
    ISBN 1-55542-429-5
    1. Employees—Training of.   2. Teaching.   3. Teachers.   I. Title.
II. Series.
HF5549.5.T7P628   1992
658.3'124—dc20   91-38692
                                                                            CIP

FIRST EDITION
HB Printing   10 9 8 7 6 5 4   *Code 9227*

The Jossey-Bass
Management Series

Consulting Editors
Human Resources

Leonard Nadler
Zeace Nadler
College Park, Maryland

CONTENTS

FOREWORD

 nstructor Excellence is a very impressive, theoretically sound, and practically helpful book on effective employee training. Based on twenty years of research in the field, Powers has developed a comprehensive set of performance standards that facilitate excellent instructor performance. This book is indispensable for instructors with all levels of experience, as well as for managers and supervisors of training programs.

With this book, the new instructor gains valuable insight into the ways adults learn and how to deliver training utilizing these principles. It analyzes the role of the instructor and details performance expectations. Powers gives the novice instructor the basic tools for getting started with confidence and for identifying the knowledge and skills needed to perform excellently.

The experienced instructor benefits from the book's study of outstanding trainers as well. Powers helps experienced trainers understand which of their instruction techniques do and do not work in the classroom and how instructors can improve on their delivery of training. Moreover, this book focuses on specific ideas and tools for being well prepared, generating meaningful participation, developing effective presentation skills, designing sequential learning experiences, using training aids to enhance learning, and evaluating course effectiveness — all of which can help the most experienced instructor to achieve greater excellence.

From this book, the supervisor or manager of training programs gains a much clearer and useful perspective of managing instructors. Powers identifies criteria and techniques for selecting good instructors and engaging them in a process of continuing self-development. He provides tips on observing instructors at work, giving constructive feedback, and recognizing and rewarding excellent performance. This text will encourage managers and supervisors to view employee training as an *instructor performance system*, rather than as a set of miscellaneous training activities.

In fact, this last point highlights what I see to be the most critical contribution of the book—the linking of all training program elements into an interactive system. As Powers eloquently points out, "Linking the components of the system produces a result like a finely tuned orchestra. While the parts may be exquisite on their own, working together they produce a result that simply cannot be achieved alone." The key goal that runs through the whole book is performance excellence, and I believe that this eminently readable book itself is an example of performance excellence.

January 1992   Malcolm S. Knowles
Professor Emeritus of Adult Education
North Carolina State University

PREFACE

In the United States alone, approximately forty million people participated in formal, employer-sponsored training in 1990 ("Training Magazine's Industry Report, 1990," 1990). The majority of these programs were delivered by instructors who had received little or no formal training on how to instruct, who do not consider themselves training professionals, and who will, in fact, leave their instructing assignment within the next two to three years. Unfortunately, there has been no authoritative system for equipping instructors to perform effectively. As a result, most instructors and most supervisors have been left on their own to deliver what is now one of the most costly solutions to business problems in this growing multibillion-dollar training industry.

Purpose of the Book

The purpose of this book, pure and simple, is to equip instructors to perform with excellence. This, in effect, is the purpose of all training—to enable people to do their jobs well or to do them better, faster, more accurately, more efficiently, or more economically than before (Nadler and Nadler, 1989).

This book is unique because it is the first to present an authoritative system for bringing about instructor excellence and because it does so systematically and thoroughly. It pinpoints standards of performance and desirable behaviors for instructors. Even more important, it presents an integrated system for selecting capable instructors; evaluating instruction;

providing feedback; and developing, recognizing, and rewarding excellent performance by instructors.

If you instruct adults, this book will enable you to deliver
training in accordance with excellent standards of performance. If you supervise instructors, this book will enable you to
implement a system for managing instructors that is guaranteed
to bring about excellence.

Regardless of whether you are a new or experienced instructor, this book will help you to develop and strengthen
your instructing skills and enable you to take responsibility for
your development, as well as for the recognition and rewards
that you receive. Regardless of how long you have been supervising instructors, this book will help you do it better. The practical,
easy-to-use concepts described here will affect the way you manage yourself and others throughout your career, regardless of
whether you remain in training or move into other fields of
work.

Although the concepts presented in this book were developed or tailored specifically for instructors and people who
manage instructors, they are useful concepts about excellence
applicable for individuals in all kinds of professions. They have
been successfully adapted and implemented by scores of people
in a wide range of businesses and organizations around the
world. Thus, if you are involved in the field of instructing adults,
this book is for you whether you work in government, education,
business, or industry.

Origins of This Book

The idea for this book was born in the early 1970s when I
brought together a team of instructors who were perceived as
outstanding performers in the classroom. Basically, I asked this
group, "What is it that you do?" In response, these instructors
began to identify the common action they took, both in and out
of the classroom, to achieve training objectives. From their
responses, we developed a list of master performance behaviors,
which were later converted into the first set of performance
standards focused on the role of the instructor. These standards,

which have evolved over the past twenty years to become the backbone of an instructor performance system, form the essence of this book.

During this time, I became associated with the National Society for Performance and Instruction (NSPI), a professional organization dedicated to promoting excellence in human performance. Through NSPI, I became acquainted with the work of Thomas Gilbert and Geary Rummler, who promoted a systematic process for solving performance problems and seizing opportunities to improve performance. They called this system *performance analysis*. I set out to capitalize on their brilliant work and, along with a staff of six, spent many years experimenting with the application of these concepts to business situations. During these years, I directed over three hundred analyses and began to see the same causes of performance problems crop up time and time again. Eventually, I translated these common causes of performance problems into a simple yet positive premise about human beings and excellence: People will perform with excellence if they

> have well-defined jobs
> are capable of doing the job
> know what is expected of them
> have the tools to do the job
> have the necessary skills and knowledge
> receive feedback on how well they perform
> perceive and receive rewards for performing as desired

In essence, this premise represents a belief system about human beings and excellence. It forms the basis for the *instructor performance system*—the system described in this book to bring about excellent instructor performance. Although the word *excellence* has become something of a buzzword, especially in corporate circles, I use it because, in addition to denoting quality, it connotes a spirit of surpassing expectations. "Instructor excellence" refers to instructors whose performance meets *and exceeds* what is expected of them. These expectations are clearly defined in this book.

Overview of the Contents

In this book, you will be introduced to a host of simple, easy-to-use, and well-integrated tools designed to enable you to implement the concepts presented here and bring instructor excellence to fruition. Chapter One focuses on how adults learn and interact and examines the impact you have on learning. It also introduces you to the instructor performance system.

Chapter Two defines the job of the instructor and identifies the skills, knowledge, qualifications, experience, and characteristics required of excellent instructors. Chapter Three provides supervisors with a set of tools to select instructors based on the skills required to successfully carry out the job. In addition, instructors and would-be instructors will learn how to assess their own skills against excellent selection criteria.

Chapter Four introduces the instructor performance standards. Here you will learn how performance standards serve to communicate expectations. These standards of excellence have been implemented in outstanding companies around the world.

Chapters Five through Eleven define and explore each of the sixty performance standards and show you how to adapt them to fit your job and your organization. Chapter Five helps you to prepare to instruct, while Chapter Six guides you to create abundant classroom participation. In Chapter Seven, you will examine the platform skills standards, and in Chapter Eight you will focus on those standards that cover course content and sequencing. Chapter Nine is intended to help you meet the standards for asking and answering questions, while Chapter Ten enables you to meet standards related to the use of training aids. Chapter Eleven will show you how to use the evaluation standards to strengthen and develop course content and your instructing skills.

Chapter Twelve focuses on helping supervisors to provide feedback that reinforces and develops excellent performance. It provides supervisors with tools to observe and document instructor performance, conduct progress reviews, handle difficult performance discussions, and complete performance appraisals. This chapter also enables instructors to assess themselves and strengthen their own performance.

In Chapter Thirteen, supervisors learn how to recognize and reward instructors in a way that improves desired performance without inflating budgets. This chapter also guides instructors to take responsibility for the recognition and rewards they receive.

In Chapter Fourteen, supervisors will learn how to develop instructors to successfully perform the instructor job and prepare for future jobs. This chapter also enables instructors to take responsibility for their own development.

Chapter Fifteen reviews the instructor performance system, summarizes the concepts presented here, shows how to use the book as a tool, and outlines the steps that instructors, supervisors, and others should begin to take to implement the ideas in this book.

Throughout the book, you will find examples drawn from outstanding companies around the world. These examples show how organizations have made use of the concepts presented in this book to attain instructor excellence. If you are an instructor, a supervisor of instructors, or a manager with an interest in performance excellence, I believe you will find great value in this book.

San Francisco, California   Bob Powers
January 1992

ACKNOWLEDGMENTS

There are many people who have contributed to this work. I would like to take my hat off to the following: my friend Jerry Arca for bringing me into Pacific Telephone Company; C. Lee Cox, for selecting me for my first training job; Allen Prestegard, for opening my eyes to good management; Michael Learned, William Truesdell, Susan Aycock-Williams, Helene Popenhager, Stan Cotrell, Robert DeCosta, Delores Williams Bullard, Joyce Botta (Schanten), Fred Garner, Robert Petillon, Liz Moore, Donald Light, Lorraine Wicks, Jeanne Nixon, and others whom I have forgotten, for contributing to the development of the instructor performance standards; Margo Murray, for introducing me to NSPI; Geary Rummler, for helping me develop into a true performance analyst; Donald Hoffman and Amy Hanan, for selecting me to head AT&T's corporate training effort; Elaine Dunst, Liz East, and, especially, my partner Anthony Ottrando, for bringing excellence to life in the workplace; William Downing, for giving me the chance to fine-tune the concepts about excellence and human beings; Donald Tosti, for creating so many of the brilliant theories on which this work is based; Steven Piersanti, for asking me to write this book; Leonard and Zeace Nadler, for serving as contributing editors to this book; Blaise Simqu, Lynn Luckow, and the Jossey-Bass staff for helping me progress through this book; and Alan Ames, my life partner, for being my personal cheerleader.

Without these people, this book would not exist.

B.P.

THE AUTHOR

B ob Powers is president of Bob Powers & Associates, Inc., a consulting firm dedicated to improving performance and enhancing life in the workplace. Founded in 1982, the firm maintains offices in Three Bridges, New Jersey, and San Francisco, California.

Powers received his B.S. degree (1963) from San Jose State College in business and industrial management and his M.S. degree (1964) from the same college in business administration.

Powers's primary focus in work has been to help people and organizations achieve desired performance results and enhance life in the workplace. He specializes in human performance systems, trainer excellence, and business planning (aligning people behind organizational goals). He has directed over three hundred consulting projects. In 1979, his AT&T training organization was recognized for outstanding achievement by the American Society for Training and Development. In 1982, his AT&T employee development organization was selected as one of four outstanding organizations in the United States by NSPI, which has also honored Powers with five presidential citations, a superior performance award, and three awards for outstanding contribution to the field of performance and instruction. Author of the *Training System Guide* (1984), publisher of the *Performance Analysis Guide* (1987), coauthor of *What Works at Work* (1988), and contributor to *Handbook of Human Performance Technology* (1992), Powers is also a frequent contributor to professional journals and publications. His instructor performance standards are used in hundreds of organizations around the world. His clients have included AT&T, British Airways, Citicorp, Dunkin Donuts, Exxon, Federal Express, General Motors, Indian Ports Authority, Oldsmobile, Pacific Telesis, the United Nations, and Yellow Freight Systems, among others.

Powers was vice president (1981-1982) and president (1984-1985) of NSPI and president of the Bay Area chapter of NSPI (1976-1977). He is a life member of the New Jersey chapter of NSPI. Since 1985, he has been listed in *Who's Who in the East* and in 1988 was added to *Who's Who in Society.* In 1986, he was profiled in *Training* magazine, one of the premier publications of the human resource development profession. Powers has also been a senior partner in Vanguard Consulting Group, a consulting firm dedicated to helping organizations successfully change. He spent fourteen years with the Bell System, where he began his career as a line manager. Before joining the Bell System, Powers was a planning officer for the Malawian Ministry of Natural Resources and a Peace Corps volunteer in Malawi.

Instructor
Excellence

PART ONE

Building a Foundation for Excellence

1

Making a Difference:
The Impact of Excellent Instructors

---

*Instructors will perform with excellence if
they are capable, have well-defined job
roles, know what is expected of them,
have the tools to do the job, and receive
feedback and rewards that reinforce
and develop excellent performance.*

This book is about instructor excellence. If you instruct adults, this book will enable you to deliver training in accordance with standards of excellence and will increase your competence and confidence. If you supervise instructors, it will enable you to implement a system of managing instructors that will produce excellence in the classroom. The practical, easy-to-use concepts described in this book will affect the way you manage yourself and others throughout your career, regardless of whether you remain in training or move into other fields of work.

In this chapter, you will look back to your own childhood experiences of learning and draw some powerful conclusions about how adults learn and the impact you can have on their learning. You will also identify how people interact and find out

3

what causes people to perform with excellence. Finally, you will be introduced to an instructor performance system designed to enable you to produce excellence in the classroom.

The Way We Learn

Think back to your early school days. Was being a student an exhilarating experience for you? Did you feel powerful, accomplished? Were you encouraged to learn and to participate? Did you know what you would be able to do as a result of what you would learn? Were you able to do something with what you learned? Were you recognized and rewarded for your achievements in the classroom? Did you want to emulate your teachers?

If, in recalling your early school days, you answered yes to all the preceding questions, were you able to go through school without being labeled a "brain" or a "teacher's pet"? If learning itself was an exhilarating experience, did you have to deal with strong, often unpleasant peer pressures, as well as pressures from family and teachers?

For many adults, their early school days were an uncomfortable time in their lives. Their experience of being a student was far from exhilarating—it was a bore. Such adults recall feeling powerless or stupid. They were encouraged to behave and be quiet rather than to learn and participate. They felt much of what they were taught was useless, and they worried about whether they would be able to do anything with what they learned. They were punished for what they did not know more often than they were rewarded for what they did know. They were referred to as "slow learners," "problem students," and "troublemakers." The last thing on earth they wanted was to be a teacher.

These experiences are ones that many adults bring with them into the classroom, and they are experiences that you must grasp if you are to successfully train adults. For many adults, walking into a training room is reminiscent of their early school days. They are generally expected to sit quietly, for much too long, in chairs that are often too small or too hard. Worse yet, you might just remind them of their third-grade teacher—the one who seemed to have it in for them. They may feel uneasy or anxious about work or home, and they may fear that they're too old or too slow or too tired to learn something new. They may question if what they are about to learn will be of any use and worry about wasting their time. They may be concerned that whatever they say will be passed on and used against them, and they may fear making a fool of themselves. To top things off, they were probably forced to attend the training session.

It's easy to understand why many adults experience difficulty the moment they walk into a training room. Whether their fears are eliminated or compounded depends primarily on you, the instructor.

In a story on adult learning theory in *Training* magazine, Malcolm Knowles concludes that there is really nothing terribly special about adults when it comes to learning (Feuer and Geber, 1988). Knowles believes that adults and children are pretty much the same not only in terms of self-directedness but also in terms of their motivation, orientation, and readiness to learn. The lone distinguishing trait is the quantity and quality of their experiences. Adults bring a greater breadth and depth of experience into the classroom, and they want to be respected for it. You can do much to eliminate the difficulties adults experience in the classroom by recognizing that adults are capable learners, by respecting their experience, and by understanding how they interact.

The Way We Interact

I want to draw from an old concept, transactional analysis (Harris, 1969), to identify how people interact with one another and how these interactions can affect learning. Transactional analysis (or TA, as it is commonly called) basically describes how people communicate or interact. In simple terms, TA holds that each person communicates from any of three states, called parent, adult, and child.

The adult state is probably the easiest to understand because it has only one form. The adult state is much like a computer. Used to present facts, logic, information, reason, and

so on, the adult state is neither emotional nor judgmental. Much
of training is delivered from this state.

The parent state has two forms. The first, which is called
the nurturing parent, is helpful, encouraging, supportive, nour-
ishing, and so on. This state is used to comfort people when they
hurt, to encourage them to accomplish tasks despite their fears,
and so on. The nurturing parent plays an important role in
training because it helps participants to meet and exceed training objectives.

The other form of parent is called the critical parent. The
critical parent is picky, judgmental, opinionated, and preju-
diced. The critical parent is quick to tell people what they have
done wrong. Instructors can expect trainees to occasionally
communicate from their critical parent state. Instructors should
avoid communicating from this state themselves because doing
so seldom accomplishes the desired training results.

There are two child states I want to talk about. The first is
the creative child, the part of a person that is imaginative,
innovative, fun-loving, free, independent, excitable, and so on.
The creative child communicates with enthusiasm and strong
feeling. Training is often delivered from this state. I like to refer
to the second as the bad-seed child. This is the part of a person
that is angry, nasty, tricky, hurt, troublesome, and so on. When
the bad-seed child communicates, it is usually with strong (and
sometimes hostile) emotion. Occasionally, trainees communicate from this state. Instructors who communicate from the bad-
seed child state seldom accomplish the desired training results.

I'd like to give you some examples of how people communicate from these states. If I were to ask a hundred people to
comment on how they might use transactional analysis in the
classroom, I might expect responses communicated from each
of the above states. The adult might say, "I can apply this concept
in the classroom to monitor my own communications as well as
those of participants." The nurturing parent might say, "This is a
wonderful concept. It will enable me to help participants meet
objectives." The critical parent might say, "This concept is twenty
years old; besides, I tried using it once, and it didn't do any
good." The creative child might respond by saying, "I'm so

excited about the possibilities of using TA. I can think of dozens of occasions when I could use this information." The bad-seed child might say, "I can see how to use this stuff to really annoy my boss."

When two or more people communicate, they either speak from the same state, such as adult to adult, or from different states, such as critical parent to bad-seed child. The following is an example of two people communicating from the same state (adult to adult). The instructor says, "Have you completed your homework assignment?" and the participant responds, "Yes, I completed it last night." The following is an example of two people communicating from different states (bad-seed child to critical parent). The participant says, "I don't see why we have to waste our time studying this stuff." The instructor responds by saying, "You should pay more attention, and then perhaps you won't have these problems."

There are times when each communication state is appropriate and others when it isn't. For example, it is appropriate to use your critical parent to yell out to someone who is in immediate danger of getting hurt. Conversely, it is inappropriate in this instance to use your nurturing parent. It is appropriate to use both your adult and creative child to solve problems; it is inappropriate to use your bad-seed child to calm down a critical parent, and vice versa (as in the example immediately above).

The key to successful communications, both in and out of the classroom, is knowing when one communication state is more appropriate to use than the others. There are three significant implications for instructors of adults:

- Learning takes place for most adults when communication between instructor and learner is adult to adult.
- Learning is often facilitated when instructors communicate from their creative child or their nurturing parent.
- Learning seldom occurs when instructors communicate from their critical parent or bad-seed child.

Again, think back to your early school days and recall a teacher who made learning an exciting experience for you.

From what communication states did this teacher instruct? I suspect your answer will include adult, creative child, and probably nurturing parent. It is difficult to imagine learning taking place without communication from the adult state, as the adult is the transmitter of information, facts, data, rationales, and so on. I suspect, if the learning experience was exciting, that your teacher communicated excitement, which stems from the creative child. I imagine this teacher also encouraged and supported you in the process of learning—and encouragement and support come from the nurturing parent.

Now recall a teacher who made learning a disaster for you and ask yourself what communication states this instructor used. I bet that your answer includes critical parent. Did the experience cause you to feel angry, frustrated, foolish, or stupid? Did you feel like a bad child? The critical parent generally brings out the worst in people because it elicits the bad-seed child, just as the bad-seed child elicits the critical parent.

You can draw some valid conclusions about adult learning from your own childhood learning experiences. Just like children, adults respond well to instructors who communicate from their adult, creative child, and nurturing parent states. Unlike children, who have little power in the classroom, most adults simply won't sit still for instructors who communicate from their critical parent or bad-seed child.

Achieving Excellent Performance

Over the past twenty years, I have developed a simple premise about human beings and excellence. It says that people will perform with excellence if they have well-defined jobs, are capable of doing the job, know what is expected of them, have the tools to do the job, have the necessary skills and knowledge, receive feedback on how well they perform, and perceive and receive rewards for performing as desired. This premise underlies the instructor performance system, which is a method of helping instructors to perform with excellence. The instructor performance system has seven basic components: job definition, selection, performance expectations, job tools, training, feedback, and rewards. Let's take a look at how each of these components derives from the initial premise.

Job definition is the component that defines responsibility for work. A good job definition is derived from an organization's mission or goals. It identifies areas of responsibility for attaining those goals; describes the skills, knowledge, qualifications, experience, and characteristics required to successfully carry out the job; and forms the basis for establishing performance expectations.

Selection is a system of choosing capable people to carry out a job. A good selection system draws from the job definition. It assesses candidates' skills, knowledge, qualifications, experience, and characteristics; matches these with the capabilities required to carry out the job; and selects candidates capable of successfully performing the job.

Performance standards, management by objectives, and target setting are different processes to define *performance expectations*, which also stem from the job definition. Performance standards are minimal levels of acceptable performance, while objectives and targets are statements of intended accomplishments. People will perform with excellence if they know what is expected of them.

Job tools are the resources available to reach performance expectations. These include equipment, manuals, procedures, and so on. Adequate tools ensure that people have the means to carry out their responsibilities efficiently and effectively.

Training equips people to perform as desired. A good training system will give people the skills and knowledge required to carry out their job.

Feedback is the process of letting people know how well they are meeting performance expectations. It includes observing, measuring, and documenting performance. A good feedback system reinforces desired performance and improves performance that does not meet expectations.

Rewards can be given when someone meets or exceeds performance expectations. Traditional job rewards include compensation, recognition, development, lateral moves, promotions, and so on. A good reward system matches the rewards to results and ensures that the rewards given are perceived to be of value by the recipient.

Each component of a performance system must be linked to the others if the system is to be successful. If you take another look at the above descriptions, you'll notice that the components are all interdependent. For example, the training component ensures that people have the skills and knowledge to do the job, the feedback component lets people know how well they are doing the job, and so on. Linking the components of the system produces a result like a finely tuned orchestra. While the parts may be exquisite on their own, working together they produce a result that simply cannot be achieved alone.

Organizations that expect excellence in performance must establish the system components necessary to support it. An incomplete performance system or one that fails to integrate all the components will not promote excellence in performance. Most organizations do have effective pieces of such a system in place. These organizations must establish the missing components and link them so that the entire system enables people to achieve the level of excellence desired. People who have worked in organizations that truly support excellence report that the experience is one they will remember for a lifetime and use as a standard for all other work experiences.

The remaining chapters of this book focus on the components of the instructor performance system. The first component—job definition—is the subject of the next chapter.

2

Articulating the Roles
and Responsibilities of Instructors

*Instructors will perform with excellence if
they have well-defined job roles.*

This chapter defines the role of the instructor and identifies the skills, knowledge, qualifications, experience, and characteristics required of excellent instructors. In fact, these requirements are built right into the instructor's job. If you're a classroom instructor you will probably find that you can use the exact job description given in this chapter. If the kind of instruction you do differs somewhat from the role described here, you can easily adapt the role to fit your precise job.

People will perform with excellence if they have a well-defined job, but many people work in organizations where jobs are not well defined. This lack of definition is one of the primary causes of performance problems. When people do not know what they are responsible for, they are unlikely to produce desired performance results. Whenever you hear someone say, "Oh, I didn't know I was supposed to do that" or "That's not part of my job," you have such a problem.

Without well-defined roles, people simply fail to take responsibility for what needs to be accomplished. They tend to

11

think of their job in terms of how they spend their time, rather than in terms of what they are expected to do or the results they are expected to produce. For example, I recently asked the vice president of a large financial organization to define his job for me. He told me that he spent his time attending meetings, taking care of items in his in-basket, supporting top management, and handling personnel problems. He made no mention of those functions for which he was paid, such as raising capital, ensuring the financial integrity of the company, and so forth. In other words, he thought of his job in terms of how he spent his time. Unfortunately, this is how most people tend to look at their work. When job roles are ill defined, people lose sight of why the job even exists. A well-defined job serves to focus people on the real purpose of their work.

What Is a Well-Defined Job?

A good job definition states what the job's function is and why the position exists. This statement stems from the mission or goals of the organization. For example, if the purpose of training is to equip people to perform their jobs, then the instructor job exists to deliver training that equips people to perform their jobs. Similarly, the course developer job exists to develop training material that enables people to perform their jobs. Each training position in some way supports the organization's mission or goals.

In a well-defined job, areas of responsibility or accomplishment are specified. This includes both major areas of responsibility, such as the responsibility to deliver training, and subordinate areas like creating trainee participation, using training aids to enhance learning, and so on.

A good job definition also identifies the requirements of the job. These include the skills, knowledge, qualifications, experience, and characteristics required to fulfill the job. *Skills* identify what people are required to do, whereas *knowledge* identifies what people are required to know. For example, instructors are usually expected to possess good organizing and planning skills. They are generally required to have knowledge of the subject matter they are instructing. *Qualifications* are conditions that must be met in order to carry out a job and usually include such things as degrees, licenses, and so on, while *experiences* are those events that people have lived through. For example, instructors who train engineers may be required to have engineering experience, while instructors who teach supervisory courses might be expected to have experience supervising people. *Characteristics* are attributes that are judged to be important in order to successfully carry out a particular job. Instructors may, for example, be required to be enthusiastic, honest, energetic, and so on.

Few training units have developed clear and accurate job descriptions. Instead, most organizations rely on vague job descriptions to define job responsibilities and requirements. This is a serious mistake. In essence, the real purpose of a good job definition is to clearly establish the functions to be carried out. Unfortunately, job descriptions are generally written to attain a certain level of pay or position. Given the opportunity, people write job descriptions as if their pay depends on it (it does!). Consequently, what is often found in a job description is an inflated statement of the importance of that job. Too often, the job description bears little resemblance to the job actually performed, and seldom is it a useful tool for instructors or their supervisors to promote excellence in performance. This book should help to change this situation.

The Role of the Instructor

Let's take a close look now at the role of the instructor. Although this chapter specifically describes the *classroom* instructor, you should be able to adapt this description to your exact job. We will approach the definition from three different angles: the reason the position exists, the instructor's area of responsibility, and the requirements of the job.

Why the Instructor Position Exists

If you look at the purpose of training—to equip people to do something—then the instructor position must, in some way, deliver training that equips people to do something. For example, in one training department the goal may be "to assist personnel in becoming better performers and producing better products." The instructor position in that department would then exist "to assist, through the delivery of instruction, personnel in becoming better performers and producing better products." The instuctor position must relate to organizational goals in order for those goals to be realized. If you are a management skills instructor, your job probably exists to deliver training that equips people to successfully manage others in order to meet organizational goals. If you are a technical skills instructor, your job probably exists to equip people to perform their work according to specified technical standards.

As companies differ, so do training groups. Some have personnel who are responsible for very specialized functions, while others have people responsible for multiple functions. For example, in some companies there are training personnel whose sole function is to deliver training; in others, instructors are expected to develop training as well as deliver it. In many small firms, one person holds responsibility for all phases of training, including performance or needs analysis, development, delivery, and evaluation. There are also organizations that make use of part-time and contract instructors and others that have training personnel spend half of their time in line or staff jobs.

Areas of Instructor Responsibility

There are three primary areas of responsbility for most instructor positions: preparing to instruct, instructing, and evaluating the results of instruction. In addition, instructors generally have a number of secondary responsibilities, including administrative and developmental tasks. Let's take a look at these responsibilities.

The first primary area of responsbility for instructors is preparing to instruct. This area encompasses all the activities an instructor must carry out before delivering a training course: reviewing course content (including objectives); developing training outlines or plans; ensuring that all materials, training aids, and classrooms are set up; reviewing trainee rosters to determine skill and knowledge levels; ensuring that any and all prerequisites have been met; sending out any preparatory materials; and reviewing previous course evaluations. The amount of time it takes to carry out these steps varies according to the kind and length of the courses you instruct.

The second primary responsibility is to instruct. This responsibility includes creating abundant participation, using good platform skills, being knowledgeable about course content and sequencing, employing effective questioning techniques, and using training aids to enhance learning. Most instructors spend the majority of their time on this responsibility, but the exact amount of time spent varies according to the length and frequency of courses taught.

The third primary responsibility of the instructor is to evaluate the results of instruction. This responsibility includes evaluating trainee performance against objectives, collecting evaluation data on course content and material, and assessing instructor performance. The time it takes to carry out this responsibility is generally minor.

In addition to these three primary responsibilities, instructors are often responsible for updating course material, conducting administrative tasks and special projects, and initiating and carrying out their own professional development.

Requirements of the Instructor's Job

The skills, knowledge, qualifications, experience, and characteristics required of excellent instructors must be clearly defined if the instructor is to successfully carry out his or her responsibilities. These requirements are also used to select excellent instructors (see Chapter Three). Let's define these requirements.

When I use the word *skill*, I am referring to those activities at which one is proficient or capable of being proficient. For example, a tennis player must be proficient at using a racket (a skill); a musician must be proficient at playing an instrument (also a skill). When I use the word *knowledge*, I am referring to the state of knowing about or understanding something, such as knowing about tennis or understanding music. When I use the word *qualification*, I am referring to those conditions that must be met in order to do something. Qualifications include degrees, licenses, and so on. When I use the word *experience*, I am referring to things one has done or events one has lived through. For example, a person who has sold automobiles possesses auto sales experience; a person who has performed in the theater possesses acting experience. Finally, when I use the word *characteristics*, I am referring to those traits that constitute a person's character, such as enthusiasm, honesty, integrity, and so on. It is important to distinguish among these requirements because, as you will see in Chapter Three, you use different methods to judge each of them.

The requirements discussed below stem directly from the responsibilities of the instructor's job. Those that are generally required are shown in italics. Whether an item is required or simply desired depends upon the nature of the job. For example, if instructors are expected to provide extensive feedback, they need to possess strong feedback skills; if the courses they teach include a wide mix of participants, they should possess the ability to manage a diverse group of people, and so on.

Skills. The level of skill required of instructors will depend upon the nature of the course and the completeness of the course material. The following list identifies and defines just the basic skills required or desired of classroom instructors:

- *Verbal skills* (ability to speak effectively)
- *Interpersonal skills* (ability to work effectively with others)
- *Leadership* (ability to lead people to accomplish objectives without creating hostility)
- *Reading* (ability to read and comprehend course material)
- *Organizing and planning* (ability to develop plans; ability to set priorities)
- *Platform skills* (ability to establish and hold eye contact, move and gesture naturally, and speak with a variety of inflections)
- *Decision making* (ability to make sound decisions given the information available)

- *Flexibility* (ability to change plans to meet objectives)
- *Analytical skills* (ability to comprehend and interpret information)
- *Problem solving* (ability to constructively handle unexpected problems)
- Feedback (ability to provide motivational and developmental feedback)
- Questioning (ability to ask questions in a way that produces a desired reponse)
- Participation (ability to get people involved)
- Initative (ability to initiate desired actions)
- Management of diverse groups (ability to successfully manage a mix of people)
- Risk taking (ability to take unplanned or risky actions to accomplish objectives)
- Writing (ability to write clearly and concisely)

Knowledge. The level of knowledge required of instructors also depends upon the nature of the course and the completeness of the course materials. In general, complex subject matter requires extensive knowledge, while simple subject matter requires minimal knowledge. Courses that have incomplete course material or that rely heavily on instructor input or expertise require instructors to possess extensive knowledge. The following list identifies and defines the areas of knowledge required or desired of instructors:

- *Subject matter* (minimal to extensive knowledge of the subject to be taught)
- *Organization* (minimal to extensive knowledge of the organizations involved)
- *Trainees* (minimal to extensive knowledge of the trainee population)
- *Adult learning* (minimal to extensive knowledge of how adults learn)
- Training (minimal knowledge of performance or needs analysis, course development, delivery, and evaluation)

Qualifications. Instructors are required to have successfully completed a good "train the trainer" course, that is, one that equips instructors to deliver training according to standards of excellence. In addition, some programs require instructors to complete specified prerequisites. These generally include courses that instructors must successfully complete before they are considered qualified to teach a particular program. As a general rule, most courses do not require instructors to possess degrees or licenses. There are exceptions, however. Whether a degree or license is required depends upon the nature of the course to be taught and agreements made with those who maintain training copyrights. Rarely should degrees be required because they generally attest to knowledge rather than skill. The following list identifies and defines the qualifications generally required or desired of instructors:

- *Train-the-trainer course* (successful completion of a course designed to deliver training in accordance with standards of excellence)
- Graduate degree (specified degree from a college or university)
- License (formal or legal permission to do something specified)
- Certificate (written statement testifying to a fact or qualification)

Experience. The experience required of instructors depends upon the kinds of courses that will be taught. For example, instructors of management courses are sometimes expected to possess some management experience. Instructors of technical courses are often expected to possess some technical experience. As a general rule, instructors are expected to model the skills taught; consequently, they are often required to successfully evidence the particular skills. The following list identifies and defines the kinds of experience typically required or desired of instructors:

- *Skills experience* (successful experience using skills being taught)

- Technical experience (successful experience in a specified technical area)
- Training experience (successful experience training adults)
- Line or staff experience (successful experience in line or staff assignments)
- Supervisory experience (successful experience managing others)
- Management experience (successful experience in a management position)

Characteristics. The traits required of instructors depend on the nature of the course material and the nature of the organization. For example, instructors who conduct experiential training are generally expected to be open, caring, sensitive, and so on. Instructors who conduct sales training are generally expected to exhibit enthusiasm and energy. A good way to identify the required characteristics of instructors is to examine the values of the organization itself. The following list identifies and defines the characteristics generally required or desired of classroom instructors:

- Energy (capacity for doing work and overcoming obstacles)
- Enthusiasm (eagerness and a visibly high level of interest in the subject matter)
- Commitment (ability to keep agreements and meet deadlines)
- Integrity (honesty, sincerity, and adherence to high standards)
- Self-presentation (ability to model desired behaviors)
- Self-management (capacity to work effectively with minimal supervision)
- Self-objectivity (capacity to seek and accept feedback)

Defining Your Role as an Instructor

A well-defined job is an essential part of a good performance system. You can define the role of the instructor in your organization by adapting the requirements given above to fit your exact needs. Exhibit 2.1 provides instructors and their supervisors

Exhibit 2.1. A Well-Defined Instructor Job.

I.   In support of organizational goals (please specify), this position
     exists to deliver training to enable people to (please specify).
II. This position is responsible for:
     A. Preparing to instruct (state percentage of time)
         1. Reviewing course content, including objectives
         2. Developing training outline or plan
         3. Setting up classroom, equipment, training aids, materials,
             and so forth
         4. Reviewing trainee roster to ensure that prerequisites are
             met; determining skill and knowledge levels
         5. Sending out preparatory material in advance
         6. Reviewing previous evaluations
     B. Instructing (state percentage of time)
         1. Garnering adequate participation
         2. Using good platform skills
         3. Disseminating information in appropriate sequence
         4. Employing appropriate questioning techniques
         5. Using training aids to enhance learning
     C. Evaluating (state percentage of time)
         1. Evaluating trainee performance
         2. Evaluating course content
         3. Evaluating instructor performance
     D. Updating course material (state percentage of time)
     E. Managing administrative and special projects (state percentage
         of time)
     F. Initiating and carrying out professional development (state
         percentage of time)
III. The skills, knowledge, qualifications, experience, and characteristics
     required or desired of this position are broken down as follows:
     A. Skills (check all that apply):
         1.   Verbal skills
         2.   Interpersonal skills
         3.   Leadership
         4.   Reading
         5.   Organizing and planning
         6.   Platform skills
         7.   Decision making
         8.   Flexibility
         9.   Analytical skills
         10. Problem solving
         11. Other (please specify)
     B. Knowledge (check all that apply):
         1.   Good subject matter knowledge
         2.   Good knowledge of company
         3.   Knowledge of trainee population
         4.   Knowledge of adult learning
         5.   Other (please specify)

Exhibit 2.1. A Well-Defined Instructor Job, Cont'd.

C. Qualifications (check all that apply):
  1. Successful completion of or willingness to participate in a train-the-trainer program
  2. Other (please specify)
D. Experience (check all that apply):
  1. Skills experience
  2. Technical experience
  3. Training experience
  4. Line or staff experience
  5. Supervisory experience
  6. Other (please specify)
E. Characteristics (check all that apply):
  1. Energy
  2. Enthusiasm
  3. Commitment
  4. Integrity
  5. Self-presentation
  6. Self-management
  7. Self-objectivity
  8. Other (please specify)

---

with a simple, easy-to-use tool to attain instructor excellence. This exhibit shows how the job supports the goals of the organization, lists the major and subordinate responsibilities of the job, and identifies the requirements of the job. It also allows you to approximate the percentage of time to be spent on each area of responsibility.

To define your role as an instructor, review the purpose of the job as it is defined in this chapter and revise it to fit your exact requirements. Remember, the instructor job basically exists to enable people to do something and should tie in to the organization's mission or goals. Next, review the instructor responsibilities listed in this chapter. Select those that match your needs, adding and deleting responsibilities as appropriate. If you have other responsibilities, such as course development or evaluation, include these on your list. Assign a percentage of time to be spent on each responsibility. Finally, review the list of skills, knowledge, qualifications, experience, and characteristics to be sure that they fit your needs. If you have added to the list of responsibilities, be sure to note any additional requirements.

For example, if you added course development, you will be required to possess good writing skills. If you deleted any responsibilities, review the list of requirements and scratch out those that are no longer relevant to your job.

Once you have completed Exhibit 2.1 you will possess an invaluable tool—one that can be used to select excellent instructors. This selection process is the focus of the next chapter.

3

Selecting Instructors:
A Skill-Based Approach

Instructors will perform with excellence if they are capable of performing the job.

This chapter outlines a system to select excellent instructors. If you are an instructor, you will be able to use the tools described here to assess your own skills, knowledge, qualifications, experience, and characteristics. This assessment will be invaluable when it comes to initiating and carrying out your own development (see Chapter Fourteen). If you are a supervisor, you can use the tools described here to select individuals who are capable of performing the instructor's job. You will also be able to use this information to begin developing the selected instructors.

People will perform as desired if they are capable of doing so, but few selection processes focus on a candidate's capabilities. Instead, selection is typically based on personality rather than skills and focuses on the relationship between the selecting supervisor and the instructor candidate. In other words, selecting supervisors use the process to determine how much they like a particular candidate and to judge how likely the candidate will be to support the supervisor and gain the respect of the rest of the organization. While these goals are, in fact, legitimate, they are secondary to ensuring that candidates possess the capabilities required.

A Good Instructor Selection System

I've talked with dozens of supervisors who tell me that they have no means other than instinct to ensure that a candidate is capable of performing a particular job. The purpose of this chapter is to provide supervisors with a good system for selecting a capable instructor.

What is the basis of a good selection system? First of all, it must enable the supervisor to judge a candidate's skills, knowledge, qualifications, experience, and characteristics. For example, classroom instructors are generally required to possess good organizing and planning skills. Thus, a good selection system should enable supervisors to judge a candidate's ability to plan and organize. Making such judgments has been a difficult, if not impossible, task for most supervisors. Consequently, much of this chapter is devoted to helping supervisors make effective judgments.

A good selection system also enables supervisors to match the judgments made to the requirements for the job. For example, if a job requires strong technical knowledge, the judgments a supervisor makes about a particular candidate's technical knowledge are matched to the technical knowledge required for the job.

A good selection system enables supervisors to base their selection decisions on the match between the requirements of the job and the skills, knowledge, qualifications, experiences, and characteristics of the instructor candidates. The decision should be an easy one once the requirements have been identified and the judgments made.

A good selection system enables the supervisor to use the information gained in the selection process to initiate development of the selected candidate. For example, let's say you selected an instructor who possesses fair verbal skills for a job that requires excellent verbal skills. A good selection process will enable the supervisor to identify such discrepancies and make immediate plans to strengthen the verbal skills of the selected instructor.

The following discussion analyzes the instructor selection system in detail. There are three parts to this system: actions you need to complete prior to interviewing instructor candidates, actions to take during the instructor interview, and actions required after the interview is over. The instructor selection system is specifically designed to select classroom instructors. If you adapted the instructor job description to fit your precise needs, you'll also need to adapt the instructor selection system.

Pre-Interview Actions

There are essentially three pre-interview actions to take: announcing the open position, analyzing the pre-interview data, and preparing for the interview.

Announcing the Open Position

The purpose of announcing an open instructor position is to attract as many viable candidates as possible. A good job announcement will generally attract viable candidates. Many announcements fail to attract such candidates because they contain insufficient information to enable individuals to assess their candidacy. A good job announcement will accurately define the job and the job requirements. Consequently, the instructor job description worked out in Chapter Two is an ideal tool to announce an open instructor position because it accurately describes the job to be carried out and defines in detail the skills, knowledge, qualifications, experience, and characteristics required and desired of the candidate. This information enables interested candidates to assess their candidacy and provides candidates selected for an interview with information they can use to prepare for the interview.

In addition to the information in the job description, the announcement should contain all other essential data, such as salary, work location, and so on. It should also ask candidates to submit evidence that they meet the identified requirements, and it should describe the appropriate procedures to follow. Supervisors can then use the data submitted to select candidates to interview.

Analyzing Pre-Interview Data

The purpose of analyzing pre-interview data is to enable you to select the most viable candidates to interview. Generally, the evidence candidates submit in response to announcements enables supervisors to make good judgments about qualifications, experience, and, to some extent, knowledge but seldom provides useful evidence of skills and characteristics, which must be ascertained from an interview. In judging candidates, you can use a rating scale of high to low. For example, a candidate who evidences substantial technical knowledge by virtue of an advanced technical degree but has minimum technical job experience would probably be rated high in technical knowledge and low to medium low in technical experience. When you have rated the evidence provided by all candidates, you should be able to select those you want to interview. Obviously, the candidates with the highest ratings are the ones to select for personal interviews.

In some instances, you will find that the number of candidates is overwhelming. By examining the qualifications, experience, and knowledge identified in a resume or other data sheet and matching them to the requirements of the job, you can confidently narrow your list of viable candidates to interview. When you are faced with a shortage of candidates, you'll probably want to interview each of the candidates who submitted evidence, unless there is clearly no match. The selection decision you make will be based primarily on skills rather than qualifications, experience, and so on; consequently, when faced with a short list of candidates, you may still find some who are capable of successfully performing the job.

The instructor selection form shown in Exhibit 3.1 should help you make your pre-interview decisions. Selecting supervisors should complete the first three parts of this form prior to the interview. When you have completed your pre-interview analysis and the instructor selection form, you will have a group of viable candidates to interview and you will have made some judgments about each candidate's knowledge, qualifications, and experience that will assist you to prepare and conduct skill-based interviews.

This form also serves as an excellent tool for current instructors to assess their own skills, knowledge, qualifications, experience, and characteristics against the requirements of their job. Current instructors should complete the entire form and then ask two or three peers to complete the same assessment. Select peers whom you trust to be fair and objective. Use their data and yours to note your strengths and any areas you need to develop. Particularly note any differences in the assessments and lay plans to develop those areas you would like to strengthen and those that you perceive differently from your peers. If you do not understand the information you receive from a peer, ask for clarification, remembering not to be defensive. Use the information as evidence of how someone else perceives you. Chapter Fourteen will provide you with the tools to focus your development.

Preparing for the Interview

The purpose of preparing for the skill-based interview is to enable you to conduct each interview fairly, efficiently, easily, and successfully.

Most interviews tell a lot about the interviewer and find out little about the candidate. Consequently, supervisors are often baffled when it comes time to make a selection decision. In order to select a capable instructor, you must focus on the interviewee and his or her skills. In other words, the vast majority of time should be spent finding out about the candidate's skills. Because interviewing is an infrequent occurrence, the interviewing skills of most supervisors are poorly developed. The discussion that follows will enable supervisors to conduct excellent skill-based interviews with a minimum of planning.

Exhibit 3.1. Instructor Selection Form.

Rating Scale

High: Evidence of substantial knowledge, experience; fully qualified; highly competent in skill areas; desired characteristics judged to be prevalent

Medium: Evidence of good knowledge, experience; somewhat qualified; competent in skill areas; desired characteristics judged to be somewhat prevalent

Low: Evidence of little or no knowledge, experience, qualifications; poor skills; desired characteristics judged to be lacking

In column A, list requirements for the job; in column B, write "R" if item is required, "D" if it is desired; in column C, write candidates' names or intitials at top and note rating (high, medium, or low) next to each requirement for each candidate.

Column A	*Column B*	*Column C*			
		Name	*Name*	*Name*	*Name*

Part 1: Knowledge
1.
2.
3.
4.

Part 2: Qualifications
1.
2.

Part 3: Experience
1.
2.
3.
4.

Part 4: Skills
1.
2.
3.
4.
5.
6.

Part 5: Characteristics
1.
2.
3.
4.

The planning required focuses on adapting the exercises in this chapter when making judgments about a candidate's skill levels.

Let's look at each of the skills needed for the instructor's job (see Chapter Two, especially Exhibit 2.1). For each skill, various exercises are given that you can use in a skill-based interview to judge candidates' skill levels. If you've added to the list of instructor skills, you will need to add similar exercises to enable you to judge a candidate in the skill areas you added.

Verbal skills (the ability to speak effectively). There are two ways to judge oral skills. The first and most effective is to ask the candidate to come prepared to make a short (two- to five-minute) presentation to a small group and arrange for two or three people to join you for this phase of the interview. Once the candidate has completed the presentation, judge it against the performance standards listed in Chapter Four. When it is not possible to bring in additional people, ask the candidate to make the presentation to you alone. An alternative is to simply ask candidates to tell you about successful presentations they have made and note how they prepared, whether they had a clear objective, how they presented the material, whether they achieved their objective, and what results were produced. Also note which presentation standards they met (see Chapter Four). This, coupled with your assessment of their one-on-one presentation skills, should enable you to make a good judgment in this area.

Interpersonal skills (the ability to work effectively with others). You don't really have the opportunity to work with the candidate during a short interview; consequently, the best way to gain information about candidates' interpersonal skills is to ask them to provide examples of successful collaboration with others. Note whether the examples given show them working with others or using others to accomplish a result. People with good interpersonal skills focus as much on common goals as they do on individual accomplishments. They are good listeners, keep their agreements, and keep groups on task or on purpose. People with good interpersonal skills tend to be supportive and enjoy the groups' accomplishments. Rate the candidate's response against the above traits.

A good alternative or supplemental approach is to ask candidates how they would handle certain realistic situations that require good interpersonal skills. You can use the examples listed below (under *Decision making*) and rate candidates in terms of the impact their decision or action would have on others. In other words, ask yourself if the decisions the candidates make will encourage others to take desired action or are likely to turn people off.

Leadership skills (the ability to lead others to accomplish objectives without creating hostility). These skills are much like interpersonal skills, except that here the candidate is the leader rather than a team player. Ask the candidates to offer evidence that they have successfully led a group and probe to see if the objectives were met without creating hostility. Here, too, you can use the examples listed under *Decision making*, as well as those listed under *Problem solving*. Look to see how the decisions that candidates make and the way in which they handle hypothetical problems would affect other people. Use these judgments and the evidence candidates provide to assess leadership skills.

Reading skills (the ability to read and comprehend course material). A good way to ensure that candidates possess adequate reading skills is to select a page or so of course material and ask candidates to take a moment to read the material and then, in their own words, describe the essence of the material. Look to see if the candidates communicate the gist rather than the detail of the material they have read. If you are unclear whether the candidate understands the material, use probing questions such as "In your own words, how would you describe the essence of this material to a new trainee?" or "Do you agree with the content, and, if so, why? If not, why not?"

You can also use this exercise to test for technical knowledge. For example, if you're unclear whether a candidate possesses the level of technical knowledge required to teach a particular course, select a passage of technical prose representative of the level of knowledge required and pose the same questions as above. In this way, you can confirm both reading ability and technical knowledge. You can also use these exercises to gather information about a candidate's ability to comprehend and interpret information.

Organizing and planning (the ability to establish priorities and structures and develop and carry out plans, designs, and so on). Simply ask candidates to tell you how they planned and organized for the interview. Note their responses and then use your notes to rate their planning and organizing against the following criteria: Was the planning and organizing logical, thorough, systematic, sequential, and so on? Did the candidate establish priorities? How extensive, complete, and appropriate was the planning? Overall, how well organized was the candidate for the interview?

Platform skills (the ability to establish and hold eye contact, speak with a variety of inflection, move naturally, and gesture with ease). If you've asked the candidate to make a short presentation, use the performance standards listed in Chapter Seven to judge the candidate's platform skills. When you choose not to have candidates make a presentation, use the candidate's ability to hold a one-on-one conversation to judge platform skills. For example, note eye contact, voice, gestures, and so on and rate platform skills using the following criteria: Does the candidate generally look you in the eye? Does the candidate use a variety of inflections or does the candidate speak in a monotone? Are the candidate's gestures natural and comfortable or forced? Base your judgments on these factors.

Decision making (the ability to make sound decisions, given the information available). The simple exercises identified here will give you a wealth of information about candidates' decision-making processes. These exercises also can be developed so that you can use them to judge interpersonal skills, leadership, and other skills. Create two or three realistic classroom situations and ask candidates how they would handle each one. For example, ask candidates how they would handle a student who interrupts a lecture to say that it is "a bunch of garbage." Judge each candidate's response in several ways.

First look to see if the decision the candidate makes is logical, rational, and so on. Next, anticipate how trainees would react to the candidate's decision. Would they be supportive, angered, encouraged, annoyed, relieved, frustrated, or upset? This will also give you information about the candidate's leadership, interpersonal, and problem-solving skills. For example, if the candidate told you that no one would ever say such a thing, you would probably judge the statement to be irrational, because such things do indeed happen. If the candidate said something to the effect that he or she would tell the trainee to be quiet and pay attention, it would be an example of poor leadership skills because this response would very likely elicit hostility from the remaining trainees. If the candidate responded by inquiring what the person really meant (for example, asking why the person felt that way or asking for specifics), you would probably rate their skills on the high side.

This example gives you a chance to judge how a candidate handles problems, since such disruptive behavior can easily result in a classroom performance problem. Look to see if the candidate responds defensively or nondefensively. When people respond to such statements by inquiring what the other person really means, you can comfortably rate their response as nondefensive unless the tone of voice, gestures, or other nonverbal behavior makes it defensive. At times, candidates respond to such situations by sugarcoating their hostility. In other words, they respond with a patronizing smile, tone of voice, or choice of words. For example, they might smile and say something like "I'm sure you'll understand why this is so important if you'll just stay with me through the entire lesson." In essence, what they are saying is, "Shut up and sit still."

There are numerous hypothetical situations that will give you information about candidates' decision-making skills. You might ask candidates how they would proceed with a class if two of the twelve participants hadn't arrived by ten minutes past the scheduled start time. You might ask how they would proceed with a classroom full of people and no trainee materials.

To judge decision making using these scenarios, look to see if the decision is logical, rational, and so on. Note if the candidate refuses to make a decision. Anticipate the results of the decision the candidate makes. To judge leadership and interpersonal skills, look at the impact the decision is likely to have on others. Will the decision alienate or encourage people? Is it likely to increase or defuse hostility? Will it bring people together or separate them? To judge problem solving in these scanarios, look to see if the candidate's response to problem situations is defensive, nondefensive, or sugarcoated and, based on your experience, estimate how likely the response is to reduce or solve the problem.

Flexibility (the ability to change plans to meet objectives). There are several ways to assess a candidate's flexibility. First, given any of the situations described under *Decision making*, you can ask the candidate to provide a good alternative way of handling the situation. You will find that some candidates can create several alternatives, while others stick to only one way of doing something. You will find, too, that some candidates take especially rigid positions. For example, the candidate who tells you that no one would ever interrupt a lecture to denounce it as garbage is probably exhibiting rigidity. You can stop a candidate during a presentation and ask questions and note how comfortably the candidate handles unplanned questions and how smoothly the candidate is able to continue the presentation. Of course, you can also ask the candidate to provide you with evidence of flexibility and make your assessments based upon the evidence provided.

Analytical skills (the ability to comprehend and interpret information). Few supervisors list analytical skills as an instructor requirement, yet they are essential for most classroom instructors. Much of what the instructor does is to take information developed by someone else and interpret and communicate that information to others. A good way to judge this ability in candidates is to describe a fairly complicated process, then ask candidates to take a moment to reflect on what has been said, and finally ask them to state the essence of the process using their own words. For example, I like to describe the six steps of performance analysis: identify desired performance, identify current performance, state the difference between desired and current performance, estimate the potential value of attaining the desired performance, pinpoint the causes why desired performance has not been attained, and design solutions to attain the desired performance. In addition, I like to give an example of each step. I then tell candidates to take a moment to reflect on what I've said and, in their own words, describe the six steps of performance analysis. I then note the number and sequence of the steps they recall and assess their response for clarity, logic, accuracy, and so on. I also assess any examples they give against the same criteria.

You can use any step-by-step process in this exercise to get a good sense of a candidate's analytical skills. The level of skill candidates possess in this area varies widely. Using the performance analysis example, I have had candidates who were able to state all six steps of the analysis in sequence, clearly, logically, and accurately—and provide an example of each. I've also had candidates who could recall only one or two of the steps and who were unable to describe those in a way I could understand.

Problem solving (the ability to constructively handle unexpected problems). This is a skill that most people have not developed; consequently, you may need to search for instructor candidates who can handle problems effectively. To do that, look for people who do not automatically become offensive or defensive when faced with problems. Some of the situations described under *Decision making* enable you to judge a candidate's ability to handle problems effectively. You can also ask candidates to describe a difficult work problem they have faced and follow up by asking how they handled the problem. You can then judge whether the candidates handled the problem effectively. In other words, was their response nondefensive rather than sugarcoated or defensive? Did they produce a desired result without escalating the problem? How were others affected by the way the problem was handled? (Handling classroom problems is an advanced skill and will be discussed in more detail later in this book.)

The remaining seven skills mentioned in connection with the instructor job (see Chapter Two) are generally desired rather than required of instructors. Whether or not you probe for these skills in your interview depends upon the importance you place on them and the nature of the courses the instructor will deliver.

Feedback (the ability to provide motivational and developmental feedback). There are several different kinds of feedback that may be important in the instructor's job. Motivational feedback is feedback given at the completion of a task and is intended to reinforce desirable behavior. Developmental feedback is feedback given just prior to the start of a task and is intended to mold behavior or strengthen previously observed behavior. (Chapter Twelve describes these methods of providing feedback in detail.)

There are two ways to measure a candidate's ability to provide feedback. One is to simply ask the candidate to describe having given feedback to others and then judge how well the feedback reinforced desirable behavior or reduced undesirable behavior. Another is to ask the candidate at the end of the interview to provide you (the interviewer) with feedback. In other words, ask candidates to tell you what they would like to see you continue doing and what they would like to see you do differently in future interviews. This exercise also allows you to develop an idea of their willingness to take risks and gives additional input into their flexibility, as this is an unusual interview procedure.

If you do conduct this exercise, you must be willing to hear the feedback provided and probably should respond to any feedback with a simple "thank you." If you are unclear about the feedback, ask the candidate to elaborate. You can expect that most candidates will not possess a high level of skill in providing motivational and developmental feedback. Nonetheless, providing good feedback is a desirable skill in instructors. By collecting evidence of candidates' feedback skills, you may identify individuals who have well-developed skills in this area. If you do not find candidates with well-developed feedback skills, you can begin to develop the feedback skills of the instructor you do select.

Questioning (the ability to ask questions in a way that produces a response). This is a relatively easy skill to measure. You can note the kinds of questions candidates ask, and you can ensure that candidates have the opportunity to ask questions simply by asking them what questions they have. Basically, you will be looking for people to ask open questions. An open question is one that usually begins with who, what, why, where, when, or how. Open questions produce a response far more often than closed questions, which at best elicit a yes or a no and at worst elicit no response at all. Measure the questions candidates ask against the standards listed in Chapter Nine. Although all instructors are required to possess good questioning skills, this is a skill that can be developed. As a result, it is listed as a desired rather than required skill of instructor candidates.

Participation (the ability to get people to participate). Like questioning, the ability to get people to participate is a skill that can be developed. Unlike questioning, this is a difficult skill to measure in an interview. If you do have candidates make a presentation to a small group, you can use the standards of performance listed in Chapter Six to judge if and how well each candidate gains the participation of the group. You can also ask candidates to describe a situation in which they were required to get people to participate actively and discuss how they went about it. Alternatively, you could describe a hypothetical situation in which people are not participating and ask what the candidate would do about it. In both these situations, match the responses candidates make against the performance standards in Chapter Six.

Initiative (the ability to initiate action). Because instructors generally work with minimal supervision, you will want to find instructors who have developed an ability to initiate and carry out action. There are three good ways to collect data on this skill area. One is to pose hypothetical situations that enable candidates to take action or wait for someone else to take action. For example, you might ask candidates how they would handle the following situation. Tell candidates that they are to assume they are instructing a course in which their supervisor is observing them. Three of the trainees are ten minutes late returning from lunch. The trainees who are present tell you that the missing three are looking for a parking space. Ask candidates what action they would take. Look to see if they initiate action themselves or ask their supervisor what to do. In this example, you are judging whether the candidate initiates action or looks to someone else to take action.

Another means to judge initiative is to ask candidates what they did in previous jobs to develop themselves and then probe to see if the actions they took were initiated by them or by someone else. Another method to judge initiative is to provide pairs of opposites and ask participants which they prefer in each pair. For example, do they prefer starting things (which shows initiative) or maintaining things?

Managing diverse groups (the ability to successfully manage a mix or variety of people). Whether this is a required or a desired skill depends on the mix of participants who attend your programs. If your trainee population is homogeneous, this skill is less critical than when your trainee population is heterogeneous. The best way to gather evidence here is to ask for instances in which the candidate successfully managed or worked with a wide variety of people. Look for the absence of bias on all grounds, including race, sex, religion, age, sexual preference, and so on. Probe to identify the candidate's comfort level in working with higher or lower levels of management and with people whose expertise in a field exceeds their own. I usually ask candidates whether they prefer working with people who have similar qualities or with a wide mix of people, and I follow up that question by asking why.

Risk taking (the willingness to take unplanned action to accomplish objectives). Many people simply are unwilling to take risks. Whether risk taking is a desired or a required skill depends upon the curriculum you offer. Risk taking is clearly not a valued skill in certain courses, like company safety, yet it is necessary in others, like programs on creativity or risk taking. Many of the test situations you put candidates through will give you a good sense of their willingness to take risks. For example, making a presentation to a small group is a rather risky action for people to take in an interview. Some of the decisions you ask candidates to make will also pose risks. I like to ask candidates to assess their own willingness to take risks on a scale of 1 to 10 and then ask for examples of risks they have taken. Look to see if the examples they provide match their assessments.

Writing skills (the ability to write clearly and concisely to accomplish an objective). Some courses, such as business writing, require a very high level of writing skill, while others require little if any skill in this area. If strong writing skills are required, the only real way to measure this ability is to collect evidence. I like to provide candidates with a list of the skills required for the instructor's job and ask them to assess in writing their ability to carry out the job. I then measure this work against good writing criteria. I look to see if the material was well organized and clearly and concisely stated. I look for good grammar and for clearly stated objectives. I also look to see if the points made support the stated objectives. These same criteria can be used to assess papers that you ask a candidate to submit in advance of or following an interview, which is another way to collect evidence of a candidate's writing skills. It is of little value to ask candidates to describe their writing skills, because what you will collect is evidence of their ability to communicate verbally, not evidence of their writing skills.

All of the skills listed above can be judged during an interview. If you have added to or adapted these skills, you will also need to adapt the means you use to judge them.

The first time you prepare for a skill-based interview can be time-consuming. By drawing from the exercises here, you can minimize the amount of initial preparation time. Once you have conducted a few skill-based interviews, you will futher reduce the time required to prepare. In addition, you will have an array of outstanding selection exercises that you can use for years to come. You won't be a professional assessor, but you will possess the confidence and competence to select instructors who are capable of performing the job with excellence.

The Interview Form. Once you have selected the exercises you will use to measure candidate skill levels, the final step in your preparation process is to prepare the instructor interview form (see Exhibit 3.2). This form is designed to enable you to conduct your skill-based interviews fairly, efficiently, and comfortably. It is laid out sequentially, beginning with your welcome to the candidate and ending with your closing remarks to the candidate. It provides room for you to list your exercises and hypothetical scenarios in advance of the interview, and it allows you to take notes during the interview so that you will have a record of key responses. In the next section, the details of how to use this form will become clear as we go through the interview step by step.

Conducting the Interview

There are six parts to a skill-based instructor interview. The first step is to establish a comfortable climate. Many instructor candidates will be nervous at the beginning of the interview; consequently, the selecting supervisor must be responsible for creating a safe, comfortable environment that will help to ease any tension. For most candidates, the skill-based interview will be vastly different from other interviews they may have experienced. It is important not to add any extra discomfort to what candidates may experience.

Begin by genuinely welcoming candidates and letting them know what they can expect from the interview. In other words, tell them that you will be conducting a skill-based interview, the purpose of which is to enable each of you to walk away with a clear sense of the match between skills required and skills possessed. Verify that each candidate has had the opportunity to peruse the job description, including the list of requirements. If any candidates have not seen the job description, give them enough time to read through it. Let them know that the interview may be different from what they have experienced in the past and give them a sense of the order of things to come. In other words, tell them that you intend to give them some information about the job, the organization, and so on. Then tell them you will verify the data that they have provided you, explore areas of skill, and give them the chance to ask any final questions. Also, let candidates know that you will be taking notes during the interview so that you won't forget important points they will make.

The second step in a skill-based interview is to communi-

Exhibit 3.2. Instructor Interview Form.

Name:
Phone:
Date:

1. a. Welcome candidate.
   b. Describe purpose of interview.
   c. Provide overview of interview.
2. Communicate essential information about job and company.

---

3. a. Prior to interview list   1. _____
      candidate's knowledge,   2. _____
      qualifications, and   3. _____
      experience.
   b. Verify during interview.   4. _____
   c. Note additions.   5. _____

---

4. a. Ask candidate about interest in job. Begin to check off
      characteristics noted (below).
   b. Prior to interview list all skills required. Note exercises for each.
      Record candidate's response to each exercise.

   Skill: Organization and planning   *Notes:*
   Exercise: How did you plan for this
               interview?

Skill: *Notes:*
Exercise:

Skill: *Notes:*
Exercise:

Skill: *Notes:*
Exercise:

Skill: *Notes:*
Exercise:

Skill: *Notes:*
Exercise:

Exhibit 3.2. Instructor Interview Form, Cont'd.

5. Prior to interview list all characteristics required for job. Check those observed during the interview.

1.___	7.___
2.___	8.___
3.___	9.___
4.___	10.___
5.___	11.___
6.___	12.___

6. a. Give candidate an opportunity to ask questions.
    b. Provide candidate with an assessment of his or her candidacy.
    c. Ask strong candidates to reassess their interest in the job (optional).
    d. Note any agreements made: (for example, when selection decision will be announced)
    e. Thank the candidate for coming.

Note: This is a sample interview form. It can be adapted to meet your specific needs.

cate essential information. Take five minutes or so to tell the candidate about the job, the organization, and the instructor performance system, including the standards of performance for instructors. Remember, the focus of the interview should be on the interviewee, not the interviewer. If, as the interview progresses, you want to add more information or you are convinced that you have an outstanding candidate and want to sell the person on the job, do your informing and additional selling at the close. The beginning of the interview is intended to create a comfortable climate and communicate essential information.

The third step is to verify the candidate's knowledge, qualifications, and experience. Let candidates know that you've selected them to interview because of their apparent strength in these areas. Then recap each area and ask candidates if your recap is accurate and if there is any additional information they would like to give you with regard to these areas. Make a note of any additional information you receive and then move into the skills portion of the interview.

The fourth step is to collect evidence of skill. Let candidates know what you're going to do, then do what you've said you will do. In other words, give them an idea of what's coming. You don't need to go overboard on this, however. For example, if you are going to ask candidates how they organized and planned for the interview, simply ask them. Also make notes of candidate's responses and thank them for their responses. It is important to document candidate responses as this documentation will enable you to recall who said what and help you to make and support your decisions. It may take some practice to document responses as you conduct the interview, but over time you will develop this important interviewing skill.

A good way to begin the skill portion of the interview is to ask candidates to briefly describe their interest in the job. I often close interviews by asking a slight variation of that question, such as "Now that you have a good idea of the job, how would you assess your interest in it?" Starting out by asking about a candidate's interest does several things. It gets candidates talking, allows them to express their level of interest, and begins the interview with relative ease. It also enables you to verify whether the candidate has a realistic sense of the job and gives you the opportunity to correct any unrealistic impressions. It also enables you to begin noting characteristics, such as enthusiasm, energy, lethargy, and so on.

I usually follow this opening question about interest by asking candidates what they did to plan and organize for the interview, and I note their responses. I generally sequence the rest of the interview by building toward what I perceive to be the most difficult or uncomfortable exercises. For example, I generally put such areas as handling problems and analytical skills toward the end of the interview. How you sequence your interview will depend upon your own level of comfort and, to some extent, your experience. Regardless of how you sequence your interview, it is important to use the exact same examples and exercises in each interview. The reason for this is that you will eventually be comparing candidate responses. Consequently, you must not alter the scenarios you depict. If you do, you will not be conducting a fair interview, and you will have no equitable means of comparing candidate responses. Before you leave the skills portion of the interview, ask candidates if there is any other important information you should know about their skills and record the additional data.

The fifth part of the skill-based selection process is to assess characteristics. Throughout the interview, note evidence of characteristics as you observe them. If, at the end of the interview, you recognize that you lack evidence of certain characteristics, simply ask the candidate to assess these characteristics in themselves and provide instances when they demonstrated them in previous work. Alternatively, you could ask candidates to rate themselves on a high-to-low scale relative to each characteristic required or desired. A third option is for you to state each characteristic and its opposite and ask candidates to tell you which one best characterizes them. For example, if you are looking for someone who is a good team player, ask candidates if they prefer working with a group or going it alone. By the end of the interview, you should be confident that you have enough information to judge whether a candidate possesses the characteristics required and desired.

The final step in the interview is to end it. At the close of the interview, ask candidates what questions or comments they might have. At this point you can also tell interviewees whether you perceive them to be strong candidates for the job. If you do, you can simply say, "While I still have interviews to conduct, I want you to know that you are a strong candidate for the job, and I want to thank you for being here." If you do not, you can say, "I would like you to know that I have interviewed other candidates whose skills are stronger for this particular job. I'm telling you now because I don't want you to have to wait around wondering if you have the job. I'd like to thank you for being here." This feedback should only be provided after you have conducted a few interviews. Nevertheless, it is extremely valuable because it does let people walk away with some sense of how you view their candidacy. In my experience, interviewees who are considered strong candidates appreciate knowing that, and those who are not serious contenders appreciate not having to wait weeks on end wondering if they're going to get the job.

While most candidates do appreciate this candor, some will ask for reasons why they are not considered strong candidates, and you should be comfortable responding to such inquiries. If you are not comfortable providing such feedback at the end of the interview, I suggest that you do not volunteer how you view the candidate until such time as you strengthen your confidence and skill in this area. If you are asked for this information, simply tell the candidate you will be glad to provide the information. Go through your notes and match the data you've collected against the requirements of the job. Then provide the information requested.

Another thing to do at the end of the interview is to ask those candidates whom you view as strong contenders to assess their interest in the job now that they have completed the interview. This provides one final piece of data that is sometimes useful in making the selection decision, especially if several candidates are more or less equally qualified.

End the interview by letting strong candidates for the job know when you will make your decision and by letting all candidates know when they can expect to hear from you. If you have not already done so, thank them for participating in the interview.

There may be times when you will make your selection decision during an interview. This can occur when you have fewer candidates than openings and the candidate clearly meets the requirements of the job, as evidenced by the pre-interview analysis and the information you gathered during the interview. In these instances, you may want to sell the candidate on the job. To do this, take a quick break and ask the candidate to take a few moments to think about the job. Use the time to collect your thoughts and plan how you will offer the job to the candidate. When you reconvene, let the candidate know why you think he or she would be a terrific instructor by reviewing the high level of skill, knowledge, qualifications, and so on that you have observed. Close by asking the candidate to accept the job.

At the end of each interview, give yourself some time to complete your notes and ensure that you can read and understand what you have written. Once you have conducted all your interviews, you will be prepared to complete the instructor selection form.

Post-Interview Actions

Following completion of each interview, use your instructor selection form (Exhibit 3.1) to verify or modify your rating of each candidate's knowledge, qualifications, and experience and record your judgment of their skills and characteristics, using the same high-to-low scale you used earlier. Once you have completed the instructor selection form, making the actual selection should be a fairly straightforward task. Simply select the candidate who possesses the highest ratings in required areas of skill, knowledge, qualifications, and so on. If several candidates appear equal, then examine the desired requirements and use the judgments you made in these areas to make your decision. If you still have several equal candidates, then take a look at the expressed interest of the candidates and note any differences in their desire to move into the instructor's job. If you still view your candidates as equal, cover their names on the selection form, ask some of your peers or other instructors whom they would select, and base your decision on these additional judgments.

When you have made your selection, let the candidate you selected know that you felt he or she was the best of the best and clearly capable of becoming an excellent instructor. Let the candidate know each job requirement on which he or she was judged to be highly qualified and explain how this will contribute to excellence as an instructor. Say how pleased you are that the candidate is joining your organization. When you meet, in person, let the selected candidate know of any requirements you want to see strengthened or developed. In other words, don't ignore the skills, knowledge, qualifications, and so on that you suspect require development. Most people, when selected for new assignments, are thrilled they were selected and appreciate knowing what areas they can improve upon. Frankly, they will probably be knocked out by your candor and sincere desire to see them be successful. (This area will be explored further in Chapter Fourteen.)

Let those candidates who were not selected know that you have selected someone else and be prepared to let them know why they were not selected. Your selection and interview forms (Exhibits 3.1 and 3.2) will serve as aids to provide candidates with post-interview feedback, as required.

Finally, complete any required documentation, taking care to comply with company practices and any legal requirements, such as affirmative action.

Once you have completed the instructor selection process, you will possess a tool you can use successfully for years to come. A good selection process is an integral component of a complete instructor performance system, for it ensures that instructors have the skills, knowledge, qualifications, experience, and characteristics required to do the job.

4

Communicating Expectations
for Instructor Performance

*Instructors will perform with excellence if
they know what is expected of them.*

his chapter introduces the concept of performance standards, shows how performance standards serve to communicate expectations, and links the standards to the instructor's job. People will perform as desired if they know what is expected of them, but many people work in organizations where expectations are not known or not clearly communicated. When this happens, people are unlikely to produce the desired results. Whenever you hear someone say, "Oh, I didn't know you expected me to do that" or "You never told me you wanted that done," you have a performance problem.

When people don't know what is expected of them, they often spend their time pursuing activities that are not expected (and therefore not valued). For example, I recently observed an employee spend countless hours and a significant amount of money developing a set of management systems to improve an organization's ability to report financial data. Unfortunately, senior management was quite content with the current method and had no interest in developing a new system. In fact, they were quite annoyed when they discovered how much time and money had gone into the development of the new system. Not only was the employee's work not valued, but the time and money were simply lost.

When performance expectations are not clearly defined and communicated, people lose sight of what's important. A well-defined and clearly communicated set of performance expectations lets people know what accomplishments are important and consequently helps them focus their time and energies on such accomplishments.

Performance expectations can be communicated through a number of vehicles. Management by objectives and target setting are two common examples. Less common (but very effective) are performance standards. Performance standards state minimal levels of acceptable performance, while objectives and targets state desired accomplishments. Standards let people know what is expected of them by defining desirable, observable, and measurable behaviors for each job. Performance standards also define the consistency with which the behavior is expected. For example, the word *consistently* is used here to denote behavior that is expected at least 90 percent of the time the opportunity to demonstrate the standard presents itself. Similarly, the word *generally* is used to denote behavior that is expected at least 75 percent of the time, and *occasionally* is used when performance is expected to occur at least 50 percent of the time.

I purposefully avoid using the words *always* and *never*, which are often found in lists of performance standards. In my experience, no performance is required to always occur or never occur unless a person's safety is affected or large amounts of money will be lost. Remember, performance standards are statements of minimal, not maximum, levels of acceptable performance.

Of the three primary forms of communicating expectations, performance standards are the most difficult to develop. However, unlike objectives and targets, which are usually developed annually, performance standards enjoy a long life span. They are generally developed once and reviewed periodically; consequently, they are the perfect means to communicate expectations for the job of instructor, which does not change frequently.

The sixty performance standards in Exhibit 4.1 have been introduced to dozens, if not hundreds, of organizations across North America, Europe, and Asia. They have been adapted by a wide range of industries, from airlines and automobiles to fast foods and telecommunications. It is possible that the standards will fit your company precisely. The vast majority of companies make fewer than four changes, and many make none.

Performance standards are the ideal vehicle to communicate what is expected of instructors in preparing to instruct, instructing, and evaluating instruction. You can expect these roles and the related performance standards to have a long life. This is not true of other instructor roles, such as updating course material, managing administrative and special projects, and initiating and carrying out professional development, which are apt to vary widely from year to year. When roles are likely to change, setting annual targets or objectives is a more efficient means to communicate expectations.

How to Adapt the Standards to Your Organization

The key to successfully adapting the performance standards to your organization lies in gaining the agreement of key personnel, namely, your boss, peers, and subordinates, depending upon the nature of your respective roles. Don't announce that you are going to implement the standards listed in this book. Instead, gain agreement to implement the standards. By following the steps given below, you can easily adapt the performance standards whether you are a one-person training department or a large team of training professionals.

Step 1. Read through the performance standards and reach agreement on a common understanding of what is meant by each one. Chapters Five through Eleven will help you carry out this task.

Step 2. If there is disagreement as to a definition, set the

Exhibit 4.1. Performance Standards for Instructors.

The following definitions are used:
Consistently: at least 90 percent of the time
Generally: at least 75 percent of the time
Occasionally: at least 50 percent of the time

Part One: Preparing to Instruct

A. *Preparation*
1. Instructor consistently completes preparation activities in time to meet class schedules.
2. Instructor consistently reviews course content, including course objectives, prior to start of each class.
3. Instructor consistently prepares or reviews training outline or plan to meet course objectives.
4. Instructor consistently ensures that required training equipment and training aids are set up in advance and are in proper working order.
5. Instructor consistently ensures that facilities are set up appropriately and checks environmental factors, safety, and room arrangement, to the extent possible.
6. Instructor consistently ensures that required training materials are available in time to meet class schedules.
7. Instructor consistently ensures that required supplies are set in place in time to meet class schedules.
8. Instructor consistently ensures that all pre-course material has been distributed in time to meet class schedules.
9. Instructor consistently reviews trainee roster to determine trainee skill and knowledge levels and ensure that any prerequisites have been met.
10. Instructor generally reviews previous course evaluations (as available) and other relevant data in order to strengthen own performance.

Part Two: Instructing the Class

B. *Gaining Participation*
11. Instructor generally encourages participation.
12. Instructor is consistently accessible to participants during class and immediately before and after class.
13. Instructor generally refers to participants by name.
14. Instructor generally uses positive reinforcement techniques.
15. Instructor generally reacts appropriately to both minimal and overt cues.
16. Instructor generally puts participants at ease.
17. Instructor consistently maintains control of classroom situation.
18. Instructor generally uses participants as resources.

Exhibit 4.1. Performance Standards for Instructors, Cont'd.

---

19. Instructor consistently uses nondiscriminatory language and treats participants in an unbiased way.
20. Instructor generally handles classroom problems in an appropriate manner.
21. Instructor occasionally turns negative classroom situations into positive learning experiences.

C. *Platform Skills*
22. Instructor generally manages own nervousness so as not to detract from learning.
23. Instructor generally maintains equal eye contact with trainees.
24. Instructor generally uses natural and nondistracting gestures and movements.
25. Instructor consistently speaks in a clear and audible voice, with a variety of inflections.
26. Instructor generally uses the instructor's guide and other training material as a guide and not a script.
27. Instructor generally demonstrates a positive attitude toward the subject matter.
28. Instructor consistently uses words that participants understand.

D. *Content and Sequencing*
29. Instructor consistently reviews the logistics of the course at the start of each class.
30. Instructor consistently provides content and procedure overviews at the start of each major lesson.
31. Instructor consistently provides course and lesson objectives.
32. Instructor generally provides summaries and transitions.
33. Instructor consistently provides clear and concise instructions on tests, exercises, and other activities.
34. Instructor generally adheres to a specified schedule.
35. Instructor consistently presents all material accurately, as detailed in the instructor's guide and related materials.
36. Instructor generally presents all material thoroughly, as outlined in the instructor's guide.
37. Instructor generally presents all material in proper sequence, as outlined in the instructor's guide.
38. Instructor is generally able to demonstrate flexibility by deviating from course outline and schedule when necessary.

E. *Questioning Techniques*
39. Instructor generally provides opportunities for questions and reviews.
40. Instructor generally uses open questions to solicit response from participants.
41. Instructor generally uses closed questions to end discussions.
42. Instructor occasionally uses questions to test for knowledge, skills, and attitudes.

Exhibit 4.1. Performance Standards for Instructors, Cont'd.

43. Instructor consistently provides correct and concise answers to questions asked by participants.
44. Instructor, when unable to answer questions asked, generally researches answers and reports results back to participants.
45. Instructor generally answers questions nondefensively.
46. Instructor occasionally refers questions back to participants.
47. Instructor occasionally guides participants to reach answers themselves.
48. Instructor generally handles irrelevant questions appropriately.

F. *Training Aids*
49. Instructor generally uses training aids so that they add to the learning experience.
50. Instructor generally demonstrates proficiency in using training aids.
51. Instructor generally performs minor maintenance or adjustments on training aids, as required.
52. Instructor generally uses alternative training aids, as necessary.
53. Instructor consistently follows specified safety practices in using training aids.
54. Instructor consistently follows prescribed instructions in caring for training aids.

Part Three: Evaluating Instruction

G. *Participant Evaluation*
55. Instructor consistently evaluates participant performance.
56. Instructor consistently provides feedback to participants, as required.

H. *Course Evaluation*
57. Instructor consistently reviews course feedback on all evaluations and takes appropriate action.
58. Instructor consistently refers items likely to require action to the appropriate group or individual.

I. *Instructor Evaluation*
59. Instructor consistently reviews feedback to instructor and takes appropriate action.
60. Instructor consistently evaluates own performance and takes appropriate action.

standard aside and focus on those standards where there is common agreement.

Step 3. If you come across a standard that does not apply to your organization, agree to eliminate it or adapt it to fit your situation.

Step 4. If there are performance standards missing from this list that are unique or important, add them under the appropriate headings and reach common agreement on their definition.

Step 5. Now is the time to come to agreement on those standards where agreement was not reached earlier. This is generally more easily done than you might expect. By now, the vast majority of your work is complete, and, given that all of the work done prior to this step has been based on agreement, it is likely that these areas of disagreement will be resolved satisfactorily.

Step 6. Gain the commitment of your boss, peers, and subordinates, as appropriate, to make the implementation of these standards successful and to develop a plan to use the standards to monitor and evaluate instructor performance.

Gaining agreement is the key to successful implementation of the instructor performance standards. Once you have reached agreement, you will possess another valuable tool, one that lets instructors clearly know what is expected of them.

Performance standards are the backbone of instructor excellence. The next seven chapters define each of the sixty standards of performance for instructors. They are intended to help you bring this critical component of the instructor performance system to life.

PART TWO

*Mastering the Tools
of Instructor Excellence:
Sixty Standards of Performance*

5

Being a
Well-Prepared Instructor

*Instructors will perform with excellence if
they are well prepared.*

This chapter defines the classroom preparation standards. These are the standards that communicate to instructors what they are expected to do in preparing to teach a training course.

Instructors will perform with excellence if they are well prepared. This isn't very surprising. Most people perform best when they are well prepared. When people are ill prepared, the likelihood of attaining desired performance results and meeting performance objectives is greatly diminished. Being ill prepared results in classroom problems and weakens the instructor's credibility. There are ten performance standards to help you become a well-prepared instructor, and we will look at each of these in detail.

Performance Standard 1: Instructor consistently completes preparation activities in time to meet class schedules.

This standard means that when you walk into the classroom you are ready to begin instructing; in other words, there is nothing for which you are unprepared. The remaining preparation standards (2–10) cover the primary steps you need to take to be prepared, including what to review, what to set up, and what to have available. There may be other steps you need to take, depending on whether you are a traveling instructor, on the nature of the course you teach, and on the culture of your organization. These additional items are generally detailed in your instructor's guide or training materials.

By meeting this standard, you can focus your attention where it belongs, on the participants. Meeting this performance standard is much like being prepared to host a fancy dinner party. In advance of the arriving guests, you have taken care of every conceivable detail. The food is prepared, the table set, the candles lit, the room decorated, and so forth. Having attended to these details, you are now ready to focus your attention on your guests. Instructors will perform with excellence if they consistently complete preparation activities in time to meet class schedules. The instructor preparation checklist in Exhibit 5.1 should help you meet this standard.

Performance Standard 2: Instructor consistently reviews course content, including course objectives, prior to start of each class.

Simply put, this standard means that you prepare yourself in such a way that you have a solid grasp of the content and concepts of the course you are going to teach. There is a wonderful saying in *Alice in Wonderland*: "If you don't know where you're going, any road will take you there." In the classroom, it matters where you are going; consequently, it matters which road you take. By reviewing course content you become a knowledgeable and ultimately credible guide on the road to learning.

One of the major fears of new instructors is that they won't

Exhibit 5.1. Instructor Preparation Checklist.

☐ Course content and objectives reviewed.

☐ Training outline or plan to meet course objectives developed or reviewed.

☐ Equipment and training aids set up and in working order.

☐ Facilities set up and checked out.

☐ Room arranged as planned.

☐ Training materials available (participant materials, handouts, and so on).

☐ Supplies available (pencils, pads, and so on).

☐ Pre-course material distributed.

☐ Trainee roster reviewed.

☐ Previous course evaluations reviewed.

☐ Other (please specify) _____

☐ _____

☐ _____

☐ _____

---

be credible. Being prepared is this fear's antidote. Practically speaking, boning up on course content just prior to teaching the course increases both your level of knowledge and your comfort. Meeting this performance standard is akin to reading a recipe for something you want to cook. The first time you try the recipe, you probably refer to it constantly and follow it step by step. After successfully preparing the dish several times, you probably only glance at the instructions. However, if you ignore the recipe altogether, you increase the likelihood of a poor end result.

Performance Standard 3: Instructor consistently prepares or reviews training outline or plan to meet course objectives.

Basically, this standard asks instructors to know where they are going and what path they will take to get there. Nothing in the classroom is more important than doing what is necessary to enable participants to meet course objectives; consequently, this is a standard instructors should consistently meet. Training objectives let instructors know where they are going, and training outlines or lesson plans let them know how they will get there. If no plan exists, you need to create one; if one does exist—it will usually be found in your instructor's guide or notes—it is logical that reviewing the plan will help to ensure that course objectives will be met. A couple of tools that help instructors to prepare include highlighter pens, which can be used to note major points to cover, and index or note cards, which can be used to detail material that is complicated or extremely important to cover exactly.

Meeting this standard is similar to reviewing a road map before heading out of town to drive to the home of a new friend. The map will increase the likelihood that you reach your destination efficiently.

Performance Standard 4: Instructor consistently ensures that required training equipment and training aids are set up in advance and are in proper working order.

Training equipment and training aids must be set up in advance and checked to ensure that they are in good working order. They can help participants to meet objectives, but if they are out of order, they are virtually useless and can even have a negative effect on participant learning.

A great many kinds of equipment and aids are used in training today. Training aids that are commonly used in the classroom include overhead projectors, slide projectors, video cameras, monitors and playback units, computers, easels, and flip charts. While most equipment comes with instructions, you can't depend on having easy access to those instructions. Moreover, because of the wide variety of available equipment (there may be dozens of video playback units, each with a slightly different mode of operation), you really do need to set up and check out the operation of these items in advance. The time spent in preparation can save many classroom headaches. A simple step like securing a spare projector bulb or checking what's recorded on a videotape can prevent a classroom disaster. If you know anyone who has ever bought a car without checking it out and ended up with a lemon, then you'll appreciate why you do not want to create a "training lemon." If you are a traveling instructor and someone else actually sets up the classroom, confirm in advance that this standard will be taken care of for you.

Performance Standard 5: Instructor consistently ensures that facilities are set up appropriately and checks environmental factors, safety, and room arrangement, to the extent possible.

This standard refers to the room you will use to conduct training and everything that affects the comfort of the room, such as lighting, temperature, appearance, safety, and room arrangement. What it says is that you are responsible, to the extent possible, for controlling these variables so that they support learning rather than detract from it. Even if someone else does the actual setup, the instructor is ultimately responsible for the arrangement and comfort of the room. So, if you are a traveling instructor, it's a good idea to confirm that these items will be taken care of for you.

Adequate lighting, comfortable temperatures, and clean, tidy classrooms support learning. A safe environment and appropriate room arrangements do the same thing. Out of whack, any of these factors can devastate the learning experience. Can you recall falling asleep during a movie because it was too hot or missing the action at a sporting event because you were trying to keep from freezing? When people worry about their comfort and safety, they tend to find it very difficult to focus on anything else.

There are four common types of classroom arrangement: the U shape, the classroom, the circle, and the theater. Generally, the arrangement most conducive to learning is the U shape, which looks like this:

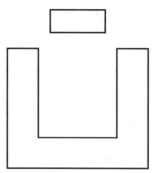

The U shape is ideal for small to medium-sized groups because it enables participants to see one another. Another popular style is simply referred to as the "classroom." This is a variation of the old schoolroom setup and is also suitable for small to medium-sized groups. The traditional classroom style calls for seating people at tables and looks like this:

For small groups, where intimacy is important to achieving objectives, a circle or semicircle is a good setup. For large groups, the theater style (row after row of chairs facing the instructor) is probably the best arrangement. Practically speaking, the room arrangement you choose will be based on your course objectives, the number of participants, the type of training you are conducting, and the availability of training space within your facility.

By ensuring that your facilities are set up appropriately, you enable people to focus their attention on what is important about being in the classroom. In other words, by consistently meeting this standard, you are helping people learn and successfully meet the course objectives.

Performance Standard 6: Instructor consistently ensures that required training materials are available in time to meet class schedules.

This standard means that you need to have materials ready before the start of each class. Materials include such items as manuals, handouts, flip charts, overhead transparencies, slides, and so forth. As with many of the other preparation standards, the primary benefit of having the appropriate materials available in time to meet class schedules is that it enables the instructor to focus on participants rather than on materials.

When these materials are not ready, you can expect to have some very anxious moments, at best, and a disaster or two, at worst. Not having the appropriate classroom materials would be akin to leading a symphony orchestra without music. While it's possible to create beautiful music, it's rather unlikely.

Performance Standard 7: Instructor consistently ensures that required supplies are set in place in time to meet class schedules.

This standard is basically the same as the preceding standard, with the focus on supplies rather than materials. Supplies include pens, pencils, pads of paper, markers, name tags, certificates, and so on. Meeting this standard helps to ensure the smooth and efficient running of the program.

Inadequate or missing supplies can put a kink in the training, from merely throwing timing off to inhibiting a participant's ability to meet objectives. How long do you imagine it would take a movie audience to become restless after the projector bulb went out if there were no spare? How long would football fans be content to watch the game without a football? It's hard to imagine either group sitting still for very long. It's just as difficult to imagine a group of trainees, restless because of a lack of supplies, staying focused for more than a short while.

Performance Standard 8: Instructor consistently ensures that all pre-course material has been distributed in time to meet class schedules.

This standard states that the instructor is responsible for ensuring that all pre-course material, including reading assignments, project work, and so on, is distributed in time to enable participants to complete the pre-course work. Meeting this standard enables trainees to begin class on an equal footing by helping to ensure that everyone enters the training with the same information or level of knowledge. Depending upon the purpose of pre-course work, meeting this standard can also provide valuable data about participants and, on occasion, can make the difference between meeting performance standards or falling short.

This standard is similar to ensuring that student drivers have a copy of the latest motor vehicles booklet before taking their driving test. When these booklets are distributed in advance, the number of student drivers who pass their driving tests is far greater than would otherwise be the case.

Performance Standard 9: Instructor consistently reviews trainee roster to determine trainee skill and knowledge levels and ensure that any prerequisites have been met.

In most instances, training is designed to be delivered to people possessing the same or similar levels of skill and knowledge. Consequently, it is the responsibility of the instructor to know as much as possible about participants prior to beginning a class. This includes knowing something about their level of skill and knowledge, and it includes knowing whether prerequisites have been met.

The most common means of ensuring that participants possess the required skills and knowledge is to check that they have successfully completed specific prerequisites, which can include certain courses, experiences, jobs, tests, and so on. In the absence of such information, instructors can often meet this standard by speaking to participants and/or their bosses, peers, or training coordinators in advance of the training. They can then use these discussions to make judgments about each participant's skill and knowledge levels. In some instances, instructors already know participants and, as a result, can use their own experience to make these judgments.

By knowing in advance the skill and knowledge levels of participants, the instructor can better gauge who may require additional help and who can be called on to act as a resource or, in some cases, expert. This information can also help instructors determine how deeply to delve into certain material and how best to pace the course. In meeting this standard, the instructor acts much like a sports coach, who reviews an athlete's abilities and previous accomplishments before planning that athlete's training.

Performance Standard 10: Instructor generally reviews previous course evaluations (as available) and other relevant data in order to strengthen own performance.

This standard asks instructors to look at their own performance prior to the start of each class and identify areas they can strengthen. Previous course evaluations, feedback from your boss, and self-assessments are all good tools to use to meet this standard. By focusing on your development just prior to delivering another program, you will better your performance in the classroom. Athletes who focus on correcting problems just prior to their next event tend to do surprisingly better than athletes who do the same sort of critical assessment just after an event. The difference is in the timing. It is useful to focus on correcting mistakes and strengthening performance when we can do something about them very shortly (the next class).

You have just reviewed the ten performance preparation standards for instructors. Like the other performance standards for instructors, these standards have been developed to help training participants meet course objectives and to help you successfully carry out your role as instructor. They let you know what you are expected to do in preparing to instruct and guide you through your preparation activities. The effort you put into preparing to instruct will pay off in the classroom.

6

Generating Abundant
Classroom Participation

---

*Instructors will perform with excellence if
they create abundant participation.*

This chapter defines the classroom participation standards. This is the first group of standards that communicate to instructors what they are expected to do while instructing.

Instructors will perform with excellence if they create abundant participation because the interchange between instructor and participants brings training to life. Moreover, trainees who actively participate tend to apply their training back in the workplace. This isn't too surprising. When people have the opportunity to join in, they often become ardent supporters of the activity at hand. Adults generally like to share their experiences. This is helpful to other participants and allows people to pass on the wisdom they have gained over the years. People also like to test their understanding of what's being discussed. Participation allows this to occur.

Not participating is a behavior people adapt to stay disconnected from a particular situation. Consequently, it is extremely important for instructors to do what they can to encourage participation. The eleven performance standards

discussed here were developed specifically to promote abundant participation.

Performance Standard 11: Instructor generally encourages participation.

Instructors are expected to encourage people to take an
active part in the class. By actively participating, trainees invest
themselves in the learning process and, as a result, have a high
success rate in meeting course objectives.

Creating participation also takes a burden off the instructor. In other words, by using participants as resources,
instructors not only gain participation but also give themselves
valuable time to think, listen, learn, and (occasionally) relax.

By bringing to life the ten remaining participation standards and by making effective use of questioning techniques
(see Chapter Nine), you will create abundant participation.
There are occasions, such as lectures, when you do not want
participation or you want minimal participation, but as a
general rule, the excellent instructor creates abundant
participation.

Performance Standard 12: Instructor is consistently accessible to participants during class and immediately before and after class.

In this standard, "accessible" means two different things.
First, it means being *physically* accessible before, during, and
after each class. A good rule to follow is to be in the classroom
and free of any tasks from fifteen to thirty minutes before the
start of each day's session and to remain there for the same
amount of time at the end of the session. You should also be
available during break and lunch periods. Being free of tasks is

key, because some participants will hold back from approaching instructors who appear to be all wrapped up in work. Making yourself physically accessible is important, particularly to participants who have problems they want to discuss and to those who simply prefer to conduct their business in private. I can think of dozens of occasions when participants have taken advantage of a break or the time before or after class to explore an idea, to discuss a problem, or to share an inspiration, any one of which can promote learning.

Second, it is important to be *emotionally* accessible during class. In other words, be sure your words and actions do not put people off. Instead, they should let participants know that it is OK — or even desirable — to approach you, to question you, and even to disagree with you.

I'd like to illustrate this by describing several ways an instructor can handle an argumentative or challenging participant. Whenever a participant challenges the instructor, the first thing that generally ensues is a dead silence. All eyes move to the instructor. If the instructor puts the challenger down, the participants will quickly conclude that it is not OK to challenge the instructor. They will probably also decide that it is not OK to argue, disagree, or even question what is being said in the classroom. Finally, they will conclude that the instructor is a jerk and probably decide to join forces with the challenger. When this happens, learning suffers.

On the other hand, if the instructor responds to the challenge positively, participants will get the message that it is OK to ask questions, raise issues, and even challenge the instructor, and they will probably conclude that there is something valuable to be learned from the class. Even if the challenge is unreasonable, the excellent instructor will not put the participant down. Instead, the instructor will try to get beyond the behavior to find out what is really troubling the participant and then take some kind of constructive action. When participants behave unreasonably and the instructor genuinely attempts to handle the situation positively, the remaining participants will conclude that the instructor is OK and the participant is a

troublemaker. Often, in this situation, the remaining participants will help the instructor deal with the troublemaker.

The point here is not to teach you how to handle a
classroom problem but rather to underline how important consistently being accessible is to the learning process. By making
yourself physically and emotionally available to participants
before, during, and after class, you will ensure that learning
takes place and training objectives are met.

**Performance Standard 13: Instructor generally refers to par-
ticipants by name.**

Most everyone agrees that using people's names is desirable. However, many do not recognize that this behavior can
threaten people as well as reinforce their participation. Consequently, it becomes important that instructors know the difference between using names to gain participation and using
names to threaten participants.

Let me pinpoint the difference. Most of you have participated in training classes where the instructor went around the
room using participants' names to run pop quizzes. The scenario goes something like this: "John, who is the author of the
xyz theory? Sally, what is the meaning of abc? Chris, where would
one look to find pqr?" As the instructor goes from participant to
participant, first John, then Sally, and next Chris comes to
attention as his or her name is called out. As soon as the
instructor has moved on to the next person, John, Sally, and
Chris tend to stop paying attention. Meanwhile, the other members of the class sit on pins and needles waiting for their turn.
This behavior threatens people. Referring to people by name is
intended to create participation, not scare them half to death.

I want to look at how the use of names can increase
participation rather than kill it. One way is to use names *after*
people have participated. For example, once John (or Sally or
Chris) has participated, say, "Thanks, John" (or Sally or Chris).

This action lets them know that you appreciate it when they comment or participate. By thanking them, you reinforce participation and avoid being judgmental.

Another effective use of names is to use them to refer back to something someone said or did earlier in the class. For example, let's say that earlier in the day John gave a very thoughtful and accurate answer to the xyz question. At the appropriate time, the instructor might say something like, "Think back to what John said earlier about the xyz theory and ask yourself what relevance his thoughtful comments have to the discussion we are having now." I will bet that not only will John continue to participate but that his face will probably light up the moment you make such a comment. Yet another effective method of using names to create participation is to draw on what you already know about participants. For example, you might say something like, "Both Sally and Chris are experts in the abc's, and we are fortunate to have them in class today." A slight variation would be to say, "Sally, I know that you have substantial experience in the abc's; how would you handle this situation?" Both examples are excellent ways of garnering participation by using names. As long as you are genuine and positive in your reinforcement, using names in this manner is an excellent way to create participation.

Referring to participants by name puts you and the participants on an equal footing. Excellent instructors refer to participants by name, except when to do so might be perceived as threatening or offensive, as in certain cultures.

Performance Standard 14: Instructor generally uses positive reinforcement techniques.

Basically, this standard means finding ways to reinforce people for participating. Most often, this simply means thanking people or acknowledging them for participating. Because positive reinforcement encourages people to further participate, it increases the likelihood that the learner will meet training objectives.

The best and easiest way of providing positive reinforcement is simply to thank people for participating. When a participant asks a question, the excellent instructor will say, "Thanks for asking that question." Similarly, participants should be thanked for making comments and for responding to questions.

Unfortunately, many people have developed a habit that actually discourages participation, even though their intention is the opposite. This is the habit of constantly using words like "excellent," "good," and "great" in responding to participants' comments or questions. In fact, it often embarrasses and sometimes even shames participants. The following scenario depicts the kind of problem that arises from this habit.

Jerry is an instructor who strongly believes in positive reinforcement. He has developed a habit of saying "excellent" to people who respond to questions, make comments, or ask questions. During class, Mary provides a thoughtful response to a question Jerry has asked about xyz. Jerry says "Excellent point" in response to Mary's comment. Mark adds his well-rounded opinion, and Jerry says to Mark, "Excellent comment." Jeff then asks a question, and Jerry responds with "Excellent question" and asks if anyone would like to answer Jeff's question. Bill raises his hand and provides a confusing and rather idiotic response. Jerry starts to say "Excellent comment" but then realizes that that is actually a foolish thing to say. He knows enough not to say "Idiotic comment," but he doesn't know what to do. The awkward silence that ensues while Jerry desperately searches his brain for an appropriate response will probably have the effect of punishing Bill and embarrassing both Bill and Jerry. It will also decrease participation by the rest of the class because the message being sent is "Don't respond unless you are absolutely sure your response is an excellent one."

Unless you are highly skilled in the nuances of positive reinforcement and can find a positive way of reinforcing confusing and idiotic responses, stick to using a simple "thank you" as your habitual response to participants. Had Jerry, in the above scenario, thanked Bill for his viewpoint and then asked the group if there were any other responses, he probably would have found someone who would have responded accurately. This action would most likely have diffused any embarrassment Bill experienced when he realized his answer was wrong.

Performance Standard 15: Instructor generally reacts appropriately to both minimal and overt cues.

Overt cues are obvious signs of a problem or potential problem and can include someone sleeping in the classroom, a fire alarm ringing, or a fistfight breaking out among participants. Minimal cues, on the other hand, are subtle signals of potential problems and include body movements (such as the head nodding that signals someone falling asleep), derogatory looks exchanged among participants or aimed at the instructor, yawning, glancing at one's watch, and so forth.

Both minimal and overt cues are signs that something is going haywire in the classroom. The instructor is expected to identify what's going on and react appropriately. While overt cues are generally easier to spot, they are also more likely to be difficult to handle. This is because by the time the cue is overt, the behavior is more likely to be a problem rather than a potential problem. Consequently, instructors who attune themselves to spotting and handling minimal cues will avoid having to deal with many difficult classroom problems.

The only way to spot minimal cues is to pay attention to what is going on in the classroom. The most effective way to do this is to use good eye contact. Good eye contact will enable you to spot anyone who nods off, which allows you to take appropriate action before the person actually falls asleep. Good eye contact will also help you see the yawners, the glarers, the squirmers, and so on. Once you have identified the cues, you can then take appropriate action, which will vary depending upon the cue. For example, if you spot someone nodding off, appropriate action would be to bring them into the discussion without embarrassing them or putting them down. There are several steps you might take to do this. Let's look at four.

First, move in the direction of the participant and see if your nearness or the increased volume of your voice gains the participant's attention. If it doesn't, ask a series of open-ended questions, the purpose of which is to get the nodder to answer one of them. As you ask each question, narrow down the group of people to whom you are directing the question. For example, first direct an open-ended question to the group as a whole. After you receive a response, turn to another part of the room (which includes your nodder) and ask another open-ended question, addressing it to "this part of the room." Continue this narrowing-down process in hopes of gaining the nodder's participation. Do *not* direct questions specifically to the nodder because that will cause embarrassment and may alienate the rest of the class.

If this narrowing-down process does not gain the nodder's participation, try a third path. This time, encourage the nodder, whom I'll call Alan, by using his name to refer back to something he said or did earlier. For example, you might say "Think back to what Alan said this morning. Who can apply what he said to the discussion at hand?" Another example would be to say something like "Both Alan and Mark work in sales; perhaps one of them will tell us how the sales department makes use of this process." Note that in both of these examples, Alan's name is used at the outset of the statement or question, not at the end. This is done on purpose so that Alan has the opportunity to hear his name, shake the cobwebs out of his head, and listen to the rest of the statement or question. By then, he may be able to make an adequate comment or response. A fourth alternative is to call a "stretch" break and give everyone, especially the nodder, the opportunity to come to life.

Taking such steps will generally gain the participation of the nodders. Occasionally, nothing you do will make a difference, and you find the nodder is now a snorer. In other words, a minimal cue has become an overt cue. While handling minimal cues requires having a wide range of approaches at your disposal, the way to handle an overt cue is generally obvious. For example, if a fire breaks out, it must be put out; if a person's safety is threatened, the threat needs to be removed. If Alan has become a snorer, it is appropriate to call a break and find out from him what can be done to gain his participation.

When instructors react appropriately to overt cues, but the problems persist, the participants must still be dealt with. The handling of classroom problems in an appropriate manner is addressed in more detail under performance standard 20. Reacting appropriately to minimal and overt cues will garner at least adequate (and usually abundant) participation. The excellent instructor will develop a grab bag of skills that can be used to react appropriately to cues. Because of the high skill level required to successfully meet this standard, it is expected generally rather than consistently.

Performance Standard 16: Instructor generally puts participants at ease.

There are many actions the instructor can take to put participants at ease. First and foremost, instructors who adhere to all the other participation standards will generally meet this standard. Putting people at ease is quite simple if you think of participants as guests. If you were at home, the first thing you would do upon the arrival of guests would be to greet them. So, greet participants when they enter the classroom. Walk up to them, shake their hands (if appropriate), and tell them you're happy to have them in your course. You will put them at ease instantly. Imagine how comfortable guests you invited to your home would be if you didn't say a word to them until they were all seated at the dinner table. Most would probably leave before dinner even began. Another thing you can do in the classroom is check periodically to make sure participants have everything they need to be comfortable. This may be uncommon behavior in the classroom, but it surely is not difficult.

You can also put people at ease if you let them know that you will do your best to help them meet objectives and enjoy the course, that what they do and say in the classroom will stay in the classroom, and that if they actively participate they will find the experience to be one of real value. Obviously, such statements must be true if you expect to be credible. Honest statements like these will reduce the tension that many participants feel when they walk into a classroom. In order to put people at ease, you have to let them know that adult learning can be vastly different from their schoolroom experiences as a child. Putting people at ease is an area in which you can have a quick and remarkably positive impact on learning.

Performance Standard 17: Instructor consistently maintains control of classroom situation.

Control, as the word is used here, does not mean that instructors lead all discussions, demonstrations, and role-playing activities, nor does it imply that instructors necessarily play any part in these situations other than being aware of what is going on and ensuring that the situations support learning and do not get out of hand. For example, if role playing is scheduled to last for fifteen minutes and spending additional time on it is likely to interfere with the day's training objectives, the instructor should ensure that participants know how much time they have remaining before they must end the role-playing session. If necessary, the instructor should see to it that they are cut off when the time is up.

Another example of maintaining control is to ensure that certain standards are adhered to. A typical scenario might look something like this. The group has just completed a rigorous role-playing session on problem solving. You are going over the session with the participants and notice that some of the comments being made are rather critical of one particular participant. You notice also that this person appears somewhat shaky.

Controlling the situation in this instance means stopping the comments before they get out of hand and hurt anyone. This can generally be done with ease. Sometimes it requires using humor; at other times it requires using effective questioning techniques. Again, the key is not to be in constant charge but to know what is going on and to take action only when necessary.

By keeping training objectives uppermost in your mind and the minds of participants and by protecting participants' self-esteem, you increase both the likelihood of participation and the likelihood that participants will meet course objectives. Participants who know that you are looking out for their welfare are likely to participate actively. If they sense that things are out of control, they will protect themselves by quickly withdrawing their participation.

Performance Standard 18: Instructor generally uses participants as resources.

This standard essentially means that the instructor is expected to call upon participants to provide answers, make key points, share experiences, and so on even when the instructor is perfectly capable of doing so. By using participants in this way, the instructor will create participation. The instructor who makes every point, provides every answer, and harps on his or her own experiences will have a tough time gaining participation. In addition, by using participants as resources, you give yourself some valuable time to think, learn, listen, and even relax. On occasion, having that kind of time can be a tremendous asset. Let me give a couple of examples.

For three sessions in a row, George had conducted a twenty-minute lecture on student learning. It was tough saying all there was to say on the subject in such a short time, and in some respects he was pleased with himself that he was able to stay on schedule. However, he was also nagged by the fact that seldom did anyone ask a question; moreover, when he con-

ducted a pop quiz on the subject, the results were poor. In his
fourth session, he decided to begin by inviting participants to
describe their own learning experiences as students. He didn't
have to ask a second question. After twenty minutes, he conducted another pop quiz. This time the results were exactly as
desired.

Cassandra was worried about teaching another safety
course. She thought students found the subject matter boring,
and she concluded that as a result they were much more unruly
than in most other classes. On this particular day, she was
experiencing some trouble with a series of very pointed questions asked by participants. Someone finally said, "Why do we
spend our time here? It seems like such a waste." Cassandra
flinched; this was the question she had hoped no one would ask.
She felt a bead of sweat on her brow and started to feel confused.
Just then, she stopped and quietly said, "Who would like to
comment on that?" It seemed as if an eternity passed before Tim
raised his hand and went on to describe an experience that cut
straight through to why people needed to be there. The person
who made the original comment said, "Thanks, Tim, I guess
you're right." At that moment, Cassandra realized that she did
not need to answer every question or make every point. She
instantly became a better instructor.

Effective questioning techniques are probably the best
tools the instructor has to encourage people to act as resources.
Open-ended questions — "How do you feel about what was just
said?" "What comments would you like to make?" — are excellent
for getting people to act as resources. (Questioning techniques
will be covered in Chapter Nine.)

**Performance Standard 19: Instructor consistently uses non-
discriminatory language and treats participants in an unbiased way.**

Basically, this standard says it is not OK to use biased
language, nor is it OK to discriminate against or act in a biased

manner toward people on grounds of color, race, gender, sexual preference, age, disability, nationality, or religion—or any other grounds, for that matter. Discrimination in the classroom is simply unacceptable. This is true even if the offender is a participant rather than the instructor; consequently, the instructor is expected to manage discriminatory or biased behavior among participants appropriately. If one person is put off because of a sexist, racist, homophobic, or other biased comment, the instructor has reduced the likelihood that all participants will meet training objectives.

Occasionally, instructors develop a habit of sexist language, sometimes without even knowing it. They tend to refer to bosses, managers, and leaders as "he" and secretaries, clerks, and typists as "she." This will generally offend someone. There are also instructors who, in an attempt to rid themselves of sexist language, use the pronouns "he" and "she" together in all references. For example, such an instructor would say, "When a manager is conducting a discussion, he or she. . . ." This behavior, when used too often, will also generally annoy someone.

A nonoffensive behavior that eliminates sexist language and is rather easy to adopt is to make nouns plural when referring to people or positions. For example, rather than saying "When a manager is conducting a discussion, he should do thus-and-so," say "When managers are conducting discussions, they should do thus-and-so." Instead of "boss," use "bosses." Instead of "secretary," use "secretaries," and so on. By making your nouns plural, you avoid sexist language altogether and reduce the likelihood of alienating participants.

Certainly most instructors and most participants avoid discriminatory or biased behavior. However, from time to time, a participant will tell a biased story or joke. As the instructor, you are expected to manage this kind of behavior appropriately. At times, you won't need to do anything because participants will stop the behavior. If the biased behavior continues, it's your job to stop it, and the best way to do that is to privately tell the participant that the behavior is not acceptable. If the behavior continues to persist, which is rare, you have a real classroom problem. Handling classroom problems is the subject of the next performance standard.

Performance Standard 20: Instructor generally handles class-room problems in an appropriate manner.

There are hundreds of problems that can crop up in the classroom, and you, the instructor, are expected to handle them in an appropriate manner. What this means is that you are responsible for ensuring that classroom problems do not get out of control, that their effect on training is minimal, and that the self-esteem of participants is kept intact. Handling class-room problems effectively will have a positive impact on learn-ing as well as increase the instructor's confidence.

The difficulty with classroom problems is that they simply do not occur often enough for instructors to become skilled in handling them. For example, how often have you seen a fistfight break out in the classroom? Fistfights do occur, but, like many of the problems you will face, they happen rarely. Most problems you will experience fall into one of three categories: disruptive participants, nonparticipants, and environmental or equip-ment problems. Exhibit 6.1 lists some of the more common problems in each of these categories.

Detailed methods of handling typical problems in each category are included in the appendix. The problems explored in the appendix are those listed with an asterisk in Exhibit 6.1. The steps for handling these problems can be applied to most, if not all, of the other problems listed.

There is one method you can employ in handling all sorts of classroom problems. That is to communicate from your adult state — and occasionally from your creative child — when you are faced with a classroom problem (see Chapter One). Because the appropriate handling of classroom problems varies from prob-lem to problem, there is no easy and constant behavior to employ except to communicate from these states. Knowing that

Exhibit 6.1. Three Categories of Common Classroom Problems.

---

1. Disruptive participants, including those who:
   talk too much
   talk incessantly with another participant*
   are argumentative
   give sharp or nasty answers
   think material is unimportant
   test the instructor's credibility
   challenge the instructor*
   ask irrelevant questions*
   make wisecracks
   make noise
   are defensive
   are offensive
   are physically disruptive
2. Nonparticipants, including participants who:
   do not participate*
   refuse to answer questions
   do not complete homework
   refuse to do assignments
   do not try hard
   sit apart from rest of class
   fall asleep or stare out the windows
   put their heads on the desk
   lie on the floor
   arrive late or leave early*
   do not return from breaks and lunch on time
3. Environmental or equipment problems, including:
   equipment failures*
   power outages
   heating problems
   air conditioning problems
   loud noises
   smoking
   poor lighting
   inadequate space
   missing materials
   a shortage of supplies

Note: Asterisks indicate classroom problems that are discussed in detail in the appendix.

you have an adult inside you capable of handling problems may be all you need to deal with whatever turns up.

I want to pass on two "Powers tips" that I believe will improve your ability to handle classroom problems — and to prevent them before they occur. The first tip is to employ a simple measurement tool called "Your Desire to Be Here." Use this tool at the outset of training and follow the steps below.

Step 1. Tell participants that they are going to rate their desire to be in the classroom using a scale of 1 (low) to 10 (high). Tell them that a 1 represents a very low desire to be here. In other words, a 1 means they would rather be anywhere else in the world. Tell them that a 10 represents a very high desire to be here, while a 5 is a perfect fence-sitter rating—they half want to be here and half don't. Tell them to pick any number from 1 to 10 and anonymously write this rating on a small piece of paper, which they should then pass to an assigned participant.

Step 2. Ask the participant to read aloud the scores. As the scores are read, post them from low to high on a flip chart. Note the range of scores and the average score and ask participants to interpret the results, being careful not to divulge their own scores. In other words, if there is a wide range of scores, ask participants to tell you why there might be such a wide range; if the average score is on the low side (a 5 or less), ask why the average might be so low, and so forth.

Step 3. Thank participants for their candor and let them know that you will do your best to make this program of value to them regardless of whether their desire to be here is a 10 or a 1.

The information you will gain in a few minutes will give you enough data to avoid most any problem participants can create. For example, if you discover that most of the participants were forced to attend, you can address that issue. If you find out that participants have personal issues that inhibit their full participation, you have the opportunity to address those issues before they become a problem. I use the "Your Desire to Be Here" measurement in every single program I teach.

The second tip I want to give you is a variation of the above. I call it the "Powers 1-2-3" scale. The Powers 1-2-3 scale is used if you don't know what's going on, or if you suspect there is a problem in the classroom but aren't sure what it is, or if there really is a problem. Let me give an example.

I once taught a course with thirty-six participants, and as I announced a break I heard one participant say to another, "Well that sure was a bunch of bullshit." I decided to spend the break in the hallway to see if this was a widespread opinion. I heard nothing. When class resumed, I asked the participants to write a number on a piece of paper that represented how they felt about the points discussed just prior to the break. I advised them that this was an anonymous exercise and gave them the following scale: a 1 meant that they found the subject matter to be of real value, a 2 meant that it was of some value, and a 3 meant that it was a bunch of bullshit. Then I arrayed the results. There were twenty-three participants who found it of real value, thirteen who found it of some value, and two who found it to be bullshit.

This exercise did a number of important things. It told me I did not have a big problem. It told the two participants who thought it was bullshit that they stood alone in their opinions. It told everyone that the vast majority of participants found the exercise valuable.

I have learned that the two most vocal groups of people are those who hate something and those who love something. The rest of the people tend to be quiet and can be somewhat more easily influenced in their opinions than either of the other two groups. Consequently, an exercise like the Powers 1-2-3 can be an effective device to calm down the extremists and is an excellent tool to unearth valuable information. For example, if the results had been different in the above exercise and I had found out that a significant number of the thirty-six participants thought the subject was bullshit, I would have been able to do something about it before it escalated into a major problem.

You can use a variation on the Powers 1-2-3 to test for pacing, interest, commitment, agreement, and so forth. By the way, the Powers 1-2-3 is an excellent tool to use out of the classroom as well.

Don't let the handling of classroom problems scare you. In time you will develop the skill to handle these problems effectively. Meanwhile, make use of the tools and tips described here and in the appendix, and I suspect you will generally handle classroom problems appropriately.

Performance Standard 21: Instructor occasionally turns negative classroom situations into positive learning experiences.

What this standard means is that you can take a classroom problem and deal with that problem in such a way that participants gain valuable learning. This is the most difficult of all standards to achieve; consequently, it is expected only occasionally.

The benefit of turning a negative event into a positive learning experience is that it is something truly valued by participants. Let me give you an example. I was instructing a class on how to instruct. In order to successfully complete the program, trainees had to demonstrate that they were capable of ensuring that participants could meet specified training objectives. They had three opportunities to do so. One participant, who was highly skilled in presentation, taught her segment. The audience found it highly entertaining—but no one met the training objectives.

I then encouraged the instructor trainee to focus the next presentation on ensuring that participants met the training objectives. On her second presentation, she was again entertaining, and again no one met the objectives. Now I had a problem, and I made two mistakes in handling this problem. I told her publicly (mistake number one) that she would not successfully complete the course unless she was able to demonstrate that participants could meet the course objectives. She became visibly upset and started to run from the room. The room was arranged so that she had to pass by me to get to the door. As she neared me I said, "Please don't leave; I know you can be a wonderful instructor." She didn't stop. As she reached me, I moved my leg to block her path (mistake number two). Realizing my mistake, I quickly pulled my leg back and let her pass. I asked one of the participants to go with her to see that she was all right, and I moved to the center of the room, not knowing exactly what to do next.

I recalled that earlier that day, during a discussion of classroom problems, a member of the class had asked me if I had ever had anyone walk out on me. I had replied no. So I said to the group, "Earlier one of you asked if I had ever had a participant walk out, and I answered no." I added, "If you recall, I told you what one might do in the event that it did happen. Now you have had the opportunity to see it happen, and I suspect you feel as bad as I do about it. I want you to know that I made two mistakes in handling this situation. . . ." I went on to describe my mistakes and let the group know what I would do to correct the situation. I did not try to hide the fact that I was upset by the situation. The result was that participation was abundant for the rest of the course, and the end-of-day evaluations were 100 percent positive. Even though I regretted the mistakes I made, I felt terrific about the feedback I received. Incidentally, I met with the participant the following morning. She stated that she wanted to complete the program, and I agreed to give her the final opportunity to meet the objectives of the program. When she made her third presentation, it wasn't entertaining, but every single person in the room met the training objectives.

Turning negative classroom situations into positive learning experiences is a standard only occasionally expected. It requires a high level of skill and probably some experience in the classroom. It is also a standard that, when met, makes the instructor feel awfully good and produces some very fine training results.

The eleven performance standards covered in this chapter are intended to enable you to create at least adequate and perhaps abundant participation in your classes. These standards, if adhered to, will encourage participants to play an active role in their learning. By developing and strengthening your skills in this important area of performance, you will be increasing the likelihood that participants will meet training objectives.

7

Building Effective
Presentation Skills

*Instructors will perform with excellence if
they use good platform skills.*

This chapter defines the standards for platform skills. This is
the second group of instructor standards that communicate
what instructors are expected to do in teaching a course. Instructors will perform with excellence if they make effective use
of eye contact, gestures, speech, and other platform skills. Let
me give a few examples.

First, can you recall sitting in a classroom where the
instructor read every single word of a text? Virtually everyone
has had that experience, and, if you're like most, it was akin to
being force-fed sleeping pills. Speaking in a constant monotone
can have the same sleep-inducing effect. If such behavior doesn't
put people to sleep, it certainly puts them off learning.

Now, can you recall an experience of being bamboozled
by an instructor? Most people have been tricked at some point
by an instructor whose platform skills were highly developed.
All most participants recall of such experiences is that they were
highly entertaining. The seven presentation standards discussed

here will enable you to deliver training in a way that improves participants' ability to learn.

Performance Standard 22: Instructor generally manages own nervousness so as not to detract from learning.

I like to define nervousness as the physical or mental manifestation of a desire to do well. You won't find this definition in the dictionary, but it's a wonderful definition because it implies that being nervous before you walk into a classroom is OK, or even desirable. I've taught hundreds of programs, and I can't recall a time I didn't experience some nervousness.

Nervousness shows itself in many ways, and each of you has your special way of being nervous. I've found that most people fall into one of six major categories depending on the predominant type of nervous behavior exhibited. As you read through these categories, note which best describes your type of nervousness. Following the list I have detailed a set of general tips for handling your nervousness, regardless of the category into which you fall. Humor can be a wonderful way of diffusing nervousness — so take what I have written here with a large grain of salt!

Categories of Nervousness

Movers and Shakers. The movers and shakers either can't sit still or can't stop shaking. The movers like to pace furiously, usually back and forth, though some do it side to side. They long for the ability to stand still in one place for more than a second. Movers should avoid training in cramped classrooms with heavy furniture.

The shakers, on the other hand, have no desire to move. They would give anything just to stop moving. Shaking the limbs is the preferred style of this group. Usually it's arms they like to shake, though sometimes it's legs and occasionally the entire body (head to toe). Shakers try everything in their power to stop shaking, but nothing seems to work. Shakers should avoid using pointers or pencils with overhead projectors.

The best way for both movers and shakers to overcome these forms of nervousness is to place their bodies (especially the moving or shaking portions) against something solid, like a desk, a chair, or a lectern. This gives movers and shakers something solid to steady them. Instead of trying to stop their shaking, shakers should exaggerate it. By doing so, they will realize that they have control over the behavior and find it easier to stop. In addition, shakers should avoid holding any objects in their hands until the nervousness disappears.

Mind Blowers. The mind blowers are those who stand up in front of the class and forget their own names. They constantly fear blanking out on this or that. You can often spot mind blowers because of the extensive notes they carry with them. Mind blowers love self-paced instruction. They should avoid teaching in rooms that do not have teleprompters.

The best way for mind blowers to overcome their nervousness is to acknowledge that their minds have blanked whenever that occurs. Saying "I've just lost my mind" will usually draw smiles or laughs from participants, allowing mind blowers to relax and carry on. This method of acknowledging nervousness has the unexpected advantage of gaining the respect of participants who admire honesty; as a result, they will often become active classroom participants.

Drippers. Drippers are adept at forming little beads of sweat on their foreheads and managing them in such a way that the beads stream down onto the bridge of the nose and then fall off the tip, creating a small puddle at their feet. Drippers also tend toward sweaty hands. They prefer fashion gear like headbands and gloves or mittens. Drippers should avoid instructing on light-colored carpets.

It might help drippers to know that the little beads of perspiration are almost never noticed by participants. If that alone doesn't comfort the drippers, then they should also know that the way to control this behavior is to have a handkerchief at their disposal and use it to wipe off the perspiration as it becomes noticeable or uncomfortable. By using a handkerchief in this way, they will be perceived by participants as trying very hard — and participants react very positively to instructors who are obviously trying to do a good job.

Gut Wrenchers. Gut wrenchers are always on the verge of throwing up. Their stomachs are in knots. This is actually a very sophisticated form of nervousness because, unless they do throw up, their nervousness is completely hidden from participants. Alert participants occasionally spot gut wrenchers because they constantly are taking antacids and tend to keep their hands on their stomachs. Gut wrenchers should avoid spicy foods.

The way to handle this form of nervousness is to follow the general tips for handling nervousness. This form of nervousness is unobservable.

Garblers. Garblers have a penchant for speaking in alien tongues. Because they are adept at phrases like "Hi, my name's been sitting on the moon," it is fun to listen to them. They often feel as if their mouths are stuffed with marbles. Like mind blowers, garblers like self-paced instruction. This leads some participants to mistake garblers for mind blowers, but they remain distinctly different creatures. Whereas the mind blowers haven't the vaguest notion of what's going on, garblers know exactly what they want to say, they just can't say it. Garblers should avoid all stand-up training except programs on sign language and other nonverbal types of instruction.

Garblers would do well to follow the advice given to mind blowers: acknowledge the problem. When words come out garbled, say something like, "I sure hope you understood what I just said, because I didn't." The resulting laugh will put you and participants at ease. If your acknowledgement also comes out garbled, use your flip chart to say the same thing; you'll probably end up with an even bigger laugh.

Cotton Mouths. Cotton mouths feel like their mouths are full of a strange kind of tar paper. They fear that without water their lips will permanently close shut, stopping even the smallest words from passing through. They are easy to spot because of a tendency to travel with large bottles of mineral water and to act hysterical if they do not have a drinking fountain within sight at all times. They also tend to lick their lips with alarming frequency. Cotton mouths love central Florida during the summer. They should avoid teaching in nonhumid climates.

Handling nervousness for cotton mouths is easy: simply have a big glass of water at your disposal and sip until your dry mouth disappears.

All forms of nervousness add up to the same thing: a desire to do well. Amazing as it seems, speaking in front of a group of people is the number one fear of Americans, which puts it above both death and taxes. Like other great fears, it cries out for a lighthearted approach. Laughter is a wonderful cure for nervousness because it discharges the nervous tension, and that is exactly what instructors need to break out of their nervousness and carry on.

Regardless of the way you exhibit nervousness, there are six general tips that are effective in reducing and eliminating all forms of nervousness.

Tips to Eliminate Nervousness

Create a Vision. Before you walk into the classroom, conduct an imaginary class in your mind. Run through the flow of the course from beginning to end, creating it, in your mind, exactly as you want it to be in real life. Remember, it's your vision, so make yourself free of nerves and, while you're at it, create participants who are anxious to be in class and who are successful at meeting course objectives. There's no reason not to add in a few sparks of instructor brilliance, too. By creating a vision, you are actually specifying desired behaviors, which is an important step in bringing them about.

Make the Classroom Your Home. Prior to the course, spend some time in the classroom making yourself comfortable with your new surroundings. Check out the size of the room, the lighting, the equipment, and so forth. Arrange the room to suit you. Remove any unnecessary distractions. Make the room feel like home so that when participants walk in, you are in comfortable surroundings.

Say Hello and Shake Hands. This simple act will rid you of most of your nervousness because it forces you to see participants as people rather than as justices of the Supreme Court. Saying hello and shaking the hands of participants will not only increase your comfort level, it will increase that of participants as well.

Take Deep Breaths. Just prior to the start of class, take a few deep breaths. As you do, relax your body from head to toe. Actually feel your shoulders drop, your arms relax, and so forth. By physically relaxing your body, you will also relax your mind.

Plant Yourself to the Ground. When it is time to begin, walk up to the front of the room, plant your two feet on the floor, and actually feel the connection of your body to the floor. Do this before you say a single word. When you feel connected, you will feel more relaxed and ready to begin.

Make Eye Contact. Before the first words come out of your mouth, make eye contact with each participant. What you will notice by looking into the eyes of participants is that they too are human beings. You will recognize that they aren't out to get you or hurt you or see you fail. In fact, they probably are just as keen as you to have a terrific experience.

These general tips should increase your level of comfort in the classroom and decrease your level of nervousness. Instructors are generally expected to manage their own nervousness so as not to detract from learning. Following the tips listed here should help you successfully meet this standard.

Performance Standard 23: Instructor generally maintains equal eye contact with trainees.

This standard means that instructors are expected to look into the eyes of each participant for a second or so. I suggest that you do this in random order so that participants do not sit there waiting for you to look at them and then nod off as soon as you do. By the way, this is a wonderful standard because it enables you to know what is going on in your classroom at all times. In addition, as I mentioned above, looking into the faces of participants can calm your nerves as well as the nerves of participants. It also signals that you care about them and are attuned to their needs.

Maintaining eye contact with participants is as effective in large groups as in small. In large groups, if you randomly move your eyes from one area of the room to another, picking one person in each area to focus on, it appears as if you are looking directly at everyone in the room. This is a technique rock stars use when they sing in large concert halls.

Performance Standard 24: Instructor generally uses natural and nondistracting gestures and movements.

The key to successfully meeting this standard lies in the word *natural*. Be aware that what is natural for one person may be absolutely foreign to another. Consequently, it is useless to expect all instructors to gesture and move alike unless you are partial to unnatural behavior. Instructors who are trained to be formal will look foolish unless that happens to be their natural style. That is just as true with instructors who have been trained to be informal.

What does work is letting instructors be their natural selves in gesturing and moving. Only then will they appear genuine to participants. Gestures and movements that are natural will enhance learning, not distract from it.

Performance Standard 25: Instructor consistently speaks in a clear and audible voice, with a variety of inflections.

In simple terms, this standard means that whenever you have something to say, say it in a way that can be heard, understood, and deemed interesting. Have you ever sat through a lecture you couldn't hear because the speaker spoke too softly or one delivered at such a loud pitch you couldn't hear yourself think? Can you recall a lecture that was delivered in a perfect monotone? If so, you probably spent the whole time wishing you could leave.

Missing the mark on any part of this standard guarantees putting people off their objectives. By speaking clearly and at an adequate decibel level, with a variety of inflections, you enhance trainee interest and learning.

Performance Standard 26: Instructor generally uses the instructor's guide and other training materials as a guide and not as a script.

This simple standard says that you shouldn't read your material to participants, regardless of the kind of material you use. The material you use to deliver your training is likely to vary from organization to organization. In some training groups, instructors deliver training using an instructor's guide or leader's guide. These documents generally provide detailed descriptions of what instructors should cover and often show which training aids to use to support each point to be made. In other groups, instructors will use some form of training notes or outlines that let them know the gist of what they are expected to cover.

Regardless of the form of your material, use it as a guide and not as a script. If you have ever sat through a lecture that was read aloud from notes by an instructor, you know why it is important to use your material only as a guide. Using your material as a script is a surefire cure for insomnia. It also severely limits the flexibility instructors require at times to meet training objectives. There are occasions when deviating from a course outline is the only way to enable participants to meet course objectives.

Performance Standard 27: Instructor generally demonstrates a positive attitude toward the subject matter.

This standard requires some definition because of the words *positive attitude*. Demonstrating a positive attitude toward the subject matter does *not* mean standing before a class full of people and telling them you think the material is the greatest thing since sliced bread, particularly if you have serious problems with the material. Conversely, it is deadly to say "I know you've heard all this stuff before but. . . ." or "I know this subject is boring but. . . ."

What demonstrating a positive attitude does mean is being careful to avoid prejudicing participants against the subject matter. Prejudicing a class in this way tends to ensure that no one will meet the course objectives. You might as well save everyone's time and money by telling the participants to go home before the class starts. I will never forget the experience of watching two instructors teach the same program and achieve vastly different results simply because of the attitudes they demonstrated toward the subject matter. The course was on company safety requirements. The first instructor kicked off the class by welcoming participants, introducing himself, and then stating, "I realize most of you don't want to be here; I can't blame you, but this is a company requirement, so you'll just have to sit here until I'm finished." He then proceeded to read an hour-long lecture on safety. The second instructor kicked off the same course by welcoming participants, introducing herself, and then stating, "I am absolutely delighted that you are here. I know that most of you have participated in previous company courses on safety, and that gives me the opportunity to draw upon your expertise to make this an especially valuable day." She then proceeded to conduct an hour-long discussion on safety.

In the first course, participants seemed visibly bored and unruly. Several failed to meet the course objectives. In the second course, participants appeared alert and interested and, without exception, met each of the course objectives. There was no difference in course content or instructor material. There was no known difference in participants. The sole difference was in the attitude demonstrated by the two instructors.

You can make an enormous difference in the results of training by demonstrating a positive attitude toward the subject matter of courses you teach. By doing so, not only will you be keeping your participants awake, but you will probably save yourself from eternal boredom. More importantly, you will significantly increase the likelihood that participants will meet course objectives.

Demonstrating a positive attitude toward the subject matter is akin to finding the proverbial glass of water half full rather than half empty or to waking up in the morning and saying "Good morning, God" rather than "Good God, morning!"

Performance Standard 28: Instructor consistently uses words that participants understand.

This standard seems self-explanatory, but it is so abused that I sometimes wonder if instructors really do have a good grasp of what it means. In simple terms, it means to speak in simple terms. In other words, use language that you know participants understand. This increases the likelihood that no one gets left behind, feels stupid, or asks what might be perceived as embarrassing questions. By using words that participants understand, you probably will come across as a good communicator and a human being, both of which will enhance your relationship with participants.

There are two common traps you should avoid because both will prevent you from meeting this objective. One is the habit of using "company-ese," the language unique to your company. The second is the habit of using big words to impress others. When I worked for a telephone company, we used a language called "telephone-ese," which is a form of verbal shorthand often using initials. We would say something like "Mary Smith was a d.a. [didn't answer]" or "I work at CTE [the Center for Technical Education]."

Every company has its own language, and, while it is unlikely to disappear overnight, instructors who use company-ese in the classroom are simply adding to problems participants might have in understanding what is being said. This is especially true of new employees, who often participate in several training programs in their first few months on the job. These people are exposed to a barrage of words, initials, and phrases that they simply don't understand and that are absolutely unnecessary.

"Big words" includes any words, phrases, or acronyms that are unnecessarily long or obscure or elaborate. Using big words is often really a means of showing off rather than an attempt at better communication. It is also ineffective in the classroom. Many years ago, I listened to a lecture in which the instructor constantly used the terms *Dk* and *De*. Upon being asked what they meant, the instructor said, "Dk means deficiency of knowledge, and De means deficiency of execution." That seemed clear enough, until I realized I didn't have a clue what those definitions meant. Upon further questioning, it became apparent that "deficiency of knowledge" simply meant that the person didn't know how to do something, and "deficiency of execution" meant they knew what to do but didn't do it. Now why couldn't the instructor just talk about not knowing how to do something rather than referring to a Dk? While it might take a couple of more words, everyone would understand the instructor.

You have just reviewed the seven performance standards related to platform skills. By developing these skills, you will bring training to life for participants, as well as help them grasp course content, which is the subject of the next chapter.

8

Adhering to Course Content and Sequencing

Instructors will perform with excellence if they are knowledgeable about course content and sequencing.

This chapter defines the content and sequencing standards for instructors. This is the third set of standards that communicate to instructors what they are expected to do in teaching a course. Being knowledgeable about content and sequencing helps instructors know what to say and when to say it. If you have ever sat through a training program with an instructor who clearly lacked the knowledge required to conduct the course, you are probably familiar with some of the many problems that can arise. Such instructors are likely to be pegged as having no credibility and are inclined to give inaccurate information—both of which reduce participants' chances of meeting objectives.

Performance Standard 29: Instructor consistently reviews the logistics of the course at the start of each class.

This standard suggests that instructors cover all relevant logistical items at the start of each class. These items can include class hours, length of course, restroom and lunch locations, homework assignments, number and length of breaks, parking and telephone arrangements, available administrative or office help, hotel accommodations, transportation, and money requirements. They can also include materials to be used, exercises to be conducted, supplies required, and so forth. The exact nature of these items will vary depending upon the length, location, and nature of the course. By letting people know what the logistical arrangements are at the outset, you eliminate a whole host of potential problems, any of which could become serious barriers to learning.

No one spends each and every day in a training class. Consequently, the routines of people are changed when they attend training, and most people don't like it when their routines are changed. It is common for people to walk into a classroom wondering if they will be able to get home on time or keep an appointment or a lunch date. They are also likely to worry about restroom facilities, luncheon arrangements, or parking. The number of worries participants can have is limitless, and these worries aren't, as is often thought, just frivolous. A luncheon appointment might be an important interview; a commitment after class might be to attend a funeral; worry about restroom facilities might stem from a health problem.

Regardless of what the logistical worry is, you can eliminate it by reviewing the items listed above. This will enable participants to focus on meeting the training objectives.

Performance Standard 30: Instructor consistently provides content and procedure overviews at the start of each major lesson.

This standard is intended to let people know where they are headed (content overviews) and how they will get there (procedure overviews). When people don't know where they are going or how they are going to get there, they can become resistant, confused, hostile, uncertain, nervous, or depressed. It's unlikely that many people would pay to join a tour that advertised, "We're not sure where we're going, but we promise we'll get you there." Likewise, it's unlikely that many participants would be willing to invest much in training that kept the destination a secret.

By letting people know where they are going and how they are going to get there, you increase the likelihood that they will get where they are headed. Content and procedure overviews are classroom road maps; they help participants start each lesson (journey) and arrive at each lesson's end as planned. In addition, they help instructors eliminate uncertainty and confusion along the way.

Performance Standard 31: Instructor consistently provides course and lesson objectives.

If content and procedure overviews let people know where they're headed and how they're going to get there, course and lesson objectives let people know what they will be able to do once they arrive. Training objectives tell people what difference training makes and enable people to measure the value of the training experience. Without objectives, it is impossible to know whether training was of any use.

Performance Standard 32: Instructor generally provides summaries and transitions.

Summaries and transitions are like checkpoints along the road to achieving training objectives. Summaries are simply reiterations of key points made at different stages along the way.

Transitions move the training from one stage to the next. Let's assume that a course is offered to equip participants to demonstrate the ten standards covered in this chapter (the objective). The instructor tells the class that the standards will be defined and demonstrated one by one (the overview). After the first standard is completed, the instructor reiterates the key points made (the summary) and then makes a statement that moves the discussion from the first standard to the second standard (the transition).

For example, to summarize the first three standards, the instructor might say something like "We've just completed the first three standards: reviewing logistical items, providing content and procedure overviews, and providing course and lesson objectives." Alternatively, the instructor might get participants to conduct the summary by asking them, "Who can tell me the first content and sequencing standard? How about the second? Who would like to tell me about the third content and sequencing standard?"

To provide a transition from the first standard to the second, the instructor might say something like "Each of you has demonstrated that you can conduct a successful review of logistical items, which is the essence of the first content and sequencing standard. Now you will have the opportunity to demonstrate the second of this set of performance standards, providing content and procedure overviews." Another version of the transition might be to say "Now that you have completed the first content and sequencing standard, let's move to the second, which focuses on providing overviews." Another effective means of making transitions is to question participants. You can say something like "What questions do you have about the logistics standard before we move on to the second standard in this group?" or "We just completed the first standard, logistical items. Who would like to tell us the essence of the second standard?"

Summaries and transitions help participants identify what is important in the maze of training material. Providing these checkpoints reinforces learning, which in turn increases the likelihood that participants will meet training objectives.

Performance Standard 33: Instructor consistently provides clear and concise instructions on tests, exercises, and other activities.

If ever there was a standard that seemed like a piece of cake but was actually rather troublesome, this is it. Providing clear and concise instructions certainly seems easy enough; after all, we give instructions frequently in and out of the classroom, usually with no difficulty. As a result, we always expect giving instructions to be easy. That is when we get into trouble. At best, poor or inadequate instructions will cause a delay; at worst, they can prevent participants from meeting training objectives.

I once had to stand up in front of a group and admit that the instructions I had given them fifteen minutes earlier not only were incorrect but also made it impossible to complete the exercise accurately. After everyone enjoyed a good laugh at my expense, I gave a new set of instructions; this time they were accurate and enabled participants to meet the objective of the lesson.

The value of providing clear and concise instructions is obvious—things run smoothly, and no one gets fouled up. Meeting this standard is easy if one recognizes how important it is to stick to the well-tested instructions written in your instructor's guide or training notes.

Performance Standard 34: Instructor generally adheres to a specified schedule.

Sticking to schedules is a delicate subject for many instructors. Inadequate or poor time management in the classroom can cause you to rush through important subjects or stretch out unimportant ones. If you have ever sat through a Friday training session that was scheduled to end at 5 P.M. and seen the looks on people's faces when the instructor announced that the session would end sometime after 6:30, you know the value of staying on schedule. I guarantee you that when timing is off, so is the likelihood that participants will meet objectives.

Staying on schedule lets participants know that you keep your commitments, tells them that their time is important to you, and generally communicates your seriousness about the program. Adhering to time commitments is greatly appreciated and generally easy to do if you follow a few simple tips. First of all, record the times you expect to be finished with each segment of training in your instructor's guide, training outline, or training notes. This will enable you to check on how well you are doing with your time plan as you move through the day. Second, note in advance those segments that can easily be shortened so that you are prepared to make an adjustment if the necessity arises. Next, avoid using open-ended questions or telling long stories if you are trying to cut discussion short. If you recognize that you may run short of time, cut down the time usually spent on breaks or lunch hours. Participants will generally be more than glad to reduce the time spent on these activities if it means getting out on time.

Performance Standard 35: Instructor consistently presents all material accurately, as detailed in the instructor's guide and related materials.

This standard advises you to use the material you have accurately; don't make stuff up. Its value is obvious. Accurate information is required to meet course objectives; inaccurate information can prevent course objectives from being met. I once observed as part of a train-the-trainer program a new instructor conduct a lecture on how to make a paper airplane fly. I noticed that the instructor paid no attention to his training notes, speaking instead off the top of his head. When it came time to fly the airplane, no one was successful. The instructor carefully looked at the planes of each participant. Unable to decipher what was wrong, he decided to repeat his lecture and started over, beginning with the first step. After the second unsuccessful attempt to fly the planes, the instructor decided to check his training notes and found the problem. He had inaccurately instructed everyone to fold their airplane's wings down rather than up, and he had forgotten to demonstrate flying an airplane. So the instructor and participants made their corrections, and on the third attempt the room was abuzz with flying airplanes. Clearly, the inaccurate instructions and failure to do a demonstration prevented participants from meeting the objective on the first two attempts.

Presenting material accurately is an easy standard to meet—unless, of course, the instructor decides to wing it instead of using the instructor's guide or training notes. Some instructors do experience problems in accurately answering questions (see performance standard 43 in Chapter Nine), but if instructors follow the information in their instructor's guide and related materials, they should be able to meet this standard with ease.

Performance Standard 36: Instructor generally presents all material thoroughly, as outlined in the instructor's guide.

This standard says don't skimp on or skip over the information contained in the instructor's guide or other training notes and materials. It doesn't mean read each word out loud; it simply means present the essence of the information in its entirety. The only exception to this rule is when you are deviating from material to meet time schedules or course objectives. (These exceptions are explained in this chapter under performance standard 38.)

By presenting all material thoroughly, you are providing

all participants with the same essential information. This will help participants meet course objectives. For example, in the airplane-making scenario discussed above, had the instructor demonstrated how to fly an airplane (a demonstration detailed in his training material), he would have been able to correct his problem immediately. One of two things would have occurred, depending on whether he had folded his own plane's wings incorrectly or correctly. Either the instructor's plane would not have flown, in which case he would have had to refer to his training notes, or his plane would have flown, in which case someone would have noticed that his plane's wings were folded differently from theirs. Either action would have corrected the problem after one attempt rather than the two it actually took.

Performance Standard 37: Instructor generally presents all material in proper sequence, as outlined in the instructor's guide.

This standard tells you to follow the training plan. Present your material in the sequence outlined in the instructor's guide. As with the previous standard, the only exceptions to this general rule occur when changing the sequence is necessary to meet time schedules or training objectives. The reason for following a planned sequence is that training is often designed in such a way that the sequence of events is an important or even essential step to achieving training objectives. For example, imagine what would happen if we failed to train pilots in the sequence of steps to follow in landing an airplane, or picture the frustration of small children who have been trained to tie their shoes before putting them on their feet. By presenting all material in the proper sequence, you increase the likelihood that participants will meet course objectives.

Performance Standard 38: Instructor is generally able to demonstrate flexibility by deviating from course outline and schedule when necessary.

In several of the content and sequencing standards, I have given you reasons not to deviate from material contained in the instructor's guide or your training notes. To meet this standard, however, you are asked to do just the opposite. On occasion, the only way to meet objectives is to deviate from the course outline or schedule. For example, if an emergency dictates that you vacate the training premises for several hours, you may have to change how you teach the material in order to meet your objectives.

On occasion, the success of a program may depend on invited guests (such as higher-level managers), and you may find yourself having to reschedule activities in order to accommodate these guests. Regardless of the reason for the change, it is incumbent upon instructors to make the change if the meeting of learning objectives is at stake. Demonstrating such flexibility is a hallmark of the excellent instructor.

You have just completed your review of the ten content and sequencing performance standards for instructors. Like the other groups of standards, these are intended to help you be successful in instructing participants. By developing your ability to effectively employ these standards, you will assist participants to gain the knowledge and skill they need to meet classroom objectives.

9

Asking and Responding to Questions

Instructors will perform with excellence if they employ effective questioning techniques.

H ave you ever wondered why some instructors get abundant participation and others get almost none? Have you ever found yourself angry because an instructor humiliated a participant for asking or answering a question? Have you ever been annoyed because you were never given the opportunity to ask questions or irritated because you were told to hold your questions till the end? The techniques instructors use to ask and respond to questions have a tremendous impact on the way participants view training. This chapter defines those techniques.

Performance Standard 39: Instructor generally provides opportunities for questions and reviews.

By providing opportunities for participants to ask questions and review key points, instructors will increase participation, reinforce key learning points, and correct misunderstandings. This simple standard can have a strong impact on whether participants meet training objectives.

As a general rule, I suggest that instructors provide frequent opportunities for participants to ask questions and review material. If you ever have sat in a classroom while the instructor droned on and on without providing a mental break or an opportunity for you to clarify a point, then you know what I mean. I highly recommend that you encourage participants to ask questions at any time.

If being that flexible is too difficult for you, you can still meet this standard by providing opportunities for questions and reviews every twenty minutes or so. Human beings simply can't listen for longer than twenty minutes without some loss of information. Consequently, if you proceed past twenty minutes, you can expect to lose participation and interest. That in turn will decrease the likelihood that people will ask questions, even given the opportunity. If they have to hold a question until later, they are likely to forget it. When people stop asking questions or can't recall the questions they wanted to ask, they are bound to be left with misunderstandings.

To meet this standard, set the stage by letting participants know that they are free to ask questions as you proceed through the course. Alternatively, you can pause every twenty minutes or so and ask, "What questions do you have?"

Performance Standard 40: Instructor generally uses open questions to solicit response from participants.

This standard is one of the most important addressed in this book because, when used effectively, it produces big results — namely, abundant responses and participation. It is also a standard that is often not met because instructors do not know how to use it. Open-ended questions force a response other than yes, no, or maybe. Open-ended questions usually begin with who, what, why, when, where, or how. For example, "What questions do you have?", "How did you arrive at that conclusion?", and "Why do you feel that way?" are all good examples of open questions. "Who would like to comment?", "When did this project begin?", and "Where did you find the information?" are also open-ended questions, though they generally produce limited, rather than full, responses.

The purpose of open questions is to open up discussion, and that is exactly what they do. Let me draw two scenarios of how questions are typically used and explore the results of each. In both scenarios, I want you to assume that you have just introduced a new and important classroom topic and that you are anxiously awaiting the discussion you expect to follow. In the first scenario, you ask participants, "Do you have any questions?" and you get no response. You then say, "Do you understand what I'm talking about?" You observe a few heads nodding up and down. You hate to leave such an important topic without discussion, so you give them one last chance and say, "Is there anything you want to ask before we move on?" No one responds. You say a few closing words and move on to the next subject.

In the second scenario, you say, "What questions do you have?" You will probably get a response with this question, but if you don't, wait a minute and then say, "If you had a question, what would it be?" You will probably get several laughs and possibly a response, but if you don't, ask, "How many of you feel you have a good understanding of the subject matter?" You can expect some or all to raise their hands, then follow up with, "Great, who will describe their understanding for me?" You will probably get one or more volunteers, but if not, pick one of those who raised their hands and ask, "Jim, would you please describe your understanding for me?" Once Jim responds, you have an opportunity to reinforce him for responding as well as an opportunity to correct the accuracy of his response. Either of these is likely to prompt additional discussion or questions. You also have the chance to turn to the group and ask, "How many of you have the same understanding as Jim?" These responses will tell you whether Jim and the group have adequate knowledge in this subject area.

I want to analyze these two scenarios. In the first, you used closed questions only and you got no response, which probably led you to believe that participants had a good understanding of the subject matter. This is a common assumption, but it is quite often a mistaken one and can have disastrous effects. In the second scenario, you used six different, yet effective, open-ended questions to gather the information you needed to safely move on to the next subject matter. First, you began with a good open-ended question: "What questions do you have?" Next, you used a follow-up question that often lightens tension and produces a response: "If you had a question, what would it be?" You then proceeded by using two open questions, both of which were intended to force specific responses. The first question — "How many of you feel you have a good understanding of the subject matter?" — forced participants to raise their hands and thus identified those who thought they had a good grasp of the subject matter. The second question — "Great, who will describe their understanding for me?" — set up an opportunity to test whether participants' knowledge was adequate. The last two questions — "Jim, would you describe your understanding for me?" and "How many of you have the same understanding as Jim?" — gave you the information you needed to make a decision about moving ahead with the course material. Let me explain. If Jim gave an adequate response and all the participants raised their hands to show that they agreed with Jim, you could safely assume that they possessed adequate knowledge to move ahead. If Jim's response was inaccurate and everyone raised their hands in agreement with Jim, you could assume that no one possessed adequate knowledge to move forward. Of course, there could be many variations on the above, depending on how many participants raised their hands. If ever you are unsure whether everyone has the knowledge to move ahead, simply continue along the same line of questioning, asking others to describe their understanding.

It is important to remember the purpose of an open-ended question: to open discussion. Open-ended questions elicit a response more often than closed questions (see performance standard 41). Consequently, if you want to start a lively discussion, elicit abundant response, or gain active participation, use open-ended questions. One way to help you develop your skill in using open questions is to ensure that you can distinguish them from closed questions. Read through the following ten questions and circle those that are open-ended.

1. Can you complete this work on time?
2. Will you be able to complete this work on time?
3. How can I help you?
4. What difference does it make?
5. Does it make any difference?
6. Do you know how to handle this problem?
7. How would you handle this problem?
8. Can you tell me how to handle this problem?
9. Where does this lead us?
10. Does this lead us in the right direction?

If you circled three, four, seven, and nine, you correctly identified the open-ended questions. All the remaining questions were closed questions because they can be answered by a simple yes, no, or maybe.

Another way to increase your use of open-ended questions is to practice translating closed questions into open-ended questions. Any of the closed questions in the previous exercise can be translated into open questions. For example, in the first question, you were asked, "Can you complete this work on time?" This question becomes an open question by asking, "How will you complete this work on time?"

If you are in the habit of using closed questions or would like to improve your ability to ask open questions, complete the following exercise. First cover up the open questions in the right-hand column. Then take a separate piece of paper and translate each closed question in the left-hand column into an open question. When you are finished, uncover the open questions and compare them with your responses.

Closed Question	*Open Question*
1. Do you understand?	What's your understanding?
2. Do you agree?	What do you agree to?

3. Is there anything else you want to know?	What else would you like to know?
4. Any questions?	What questions do you have?
5. Do you have any more questions?	What other questions do you have?
6. Could it happen again?	How could it happen again?
7. Would you ask anything more?	What else would you ask?
8. Should you continue?	How should you continue?
9. Will you remember this?	What will you remember about this?
10. Did it help you?	What was helpful about it?

There is one additional tip I want to give you before you move on to the next standard. Give participants enough time to respond to questions you ask. I have seen too many good questions go wasted because instructors answer their own questions far too quickly. It takes several seconds for participants to absorb or repeat (in their heads) the question you have just asked, and if they think they might respond, it takes another couple of seconds for them to form their response, raise their hands, and be ready to speak. The time that passes may seem like an eternity to you; in fact, it is generally a very short time (a matter of seconds rather than what may seem like minutes). Count to ten before you answer your own questions. By the time you reach ten, someone will be ready to respond.

Performance Standard 41: Instructor generally uses closed questions to end discussions.

Unfortunately, closed questions enjoy a bad reputation. The reason for this is they are generally used to open discussion rather than to close it, and, as a result, they seldom elicit the desired response. The purpose of the closed question is to close discussion, to end participation. The exception is when you use a closed question and immediately follow it with an appeal for further elaboration or an open question. For example, by asking "Do you disagree?" and immediately following that question with "Tell me about your disagreement," you are in effect doing the same thing as asking an open question. Another example is to ask something like "Do you have any thoughts on the subject?" and follow that question with "What are they?" This method of questioning has one advantage over a simple open question, which is that participants gain a moment to collect their thoughts so that when you ask the follow-up question, they are prepared to answer. Do not make the mistake of thinking that the closed question gets the response; it's the open (follow-up) question that encourages people to answer.

Closed questions are appropriate to use when you are at the end of a lecture, a discussion, or an exercise. They are also appropriate when you are ready to take a break or close for the day. If you have just completed a lecture, a discussion, or an exercise, it is perfectly appropriate to end with "Are there any questions before we move on to the next subject matter?" If you get no response, then move ahead. If you do get a response, continue to ask closed questions until you get no response. If you are going to take a break, ask, "Are there any questions before we break?" By asking the question in this manner, you are letting people know what's ahead (a break). You are also discouraging people from asking inane or irrelevant questions by implying that any questions asked might delay the break.

Using closed questions like the ones above to end discussion or wrap up the day gives participants one last opportunity to ask questions. This can be an important step for those who feel an urgent need to clarify a point or resolve an issue before moving forward.

During most classes, you reach a point where any kind of question, open or closed, elicits a response. This phenomenon is the result of having created such abundant participation that no special techniques are necessary. To help you create this kind of situation, it is important to used closed questions to end discussions and exercises, to wrap up a lesson, or to end the training day.

Performance Standard 42: Instructor occasionally uses questions to test for knowledge, skills, and attitudes.

Basically, this standard means that the instructor uses questions to determine if participants are ready to move to the next training lesson or exercise. Remember the "Desire to Be Here" exercise? (In that exercise you were asked to employ a simple measurement tool to assess participants' desire to be in the training session.) This tool is also excellent for testing attitudes. By asking the question "How would you rate your desire to be here?", you will find out if your participants are enthusiastic about being in class, if they are indifferent, or if they absolutely dread being in class. The knowledge you derive can affect how you proceed with your class. For example, in one class I instructed the average "Desire to Be Here" rating was 1.75 on a 10-point scale. There were eleven ratings of 1 and one rating of 10. I had never seen such a low average. By asking participants to interpret the low average, I discovered that all twelve participants were given less than forty-eight hours notice that they were expected to attend the course. More importantly, it was common knowledge that attending this course meant participants would be transferred from New York to Florida—a fact that not one supervisor acknowledged (one participant was thrilled with the idea of being transferred to Florida, which accounted for the one rating of 10). Needless to say, this was a group of participants with nasty attitudes. However, by asking about their desire to be in class, I collected information that enabled me to address their concerns, which in turn enabled each of them to successfully complete the program. (By the way, the end-of-course evaluation ratings were all 10s.)

On another occasion, I was hired to run a basic train-the-trainer program. Within a short time, I suspected this particular group of people possessed knowledge and skills far exceeding what I normally expected of participants in such a program. Consequently, I proceeded to ask a series of open questions that

would give me a better sense of their training skills and knowledge. "What successful training experience do you have?", "What
knowledge do you possess about developing behavioral training
objectives?", and so on. The responses I received told me that I
had a group of participants well versed in training. Consequently, I asked each participant to give a three-minute training
presentation on the subject matter of their choice. After observing their presentations, I determined that their skill levels were
high enough to do some advanced skills work.

You can test for knowledge and skill in many ways, including asking open-ended questions, asking participants to summarize lessons or key points, and asking participants to demonstrate the principles they have learned. For example, by asking
the open-ended question "What is the difference between an
open and a closed question?", you can judge whether the participant has a good enough grasp of the concept to move on to the
next standard. When you ask participants to summarize, you are
testing for knowledge. For example, by asking "Who would like
to summarize the learning points so far?", you can judge
whether participants need more knowledge in this area. When
you ask participants how they would apply knowledge to their
job, you are also testing. For example, if you ask participants
"What are three open questions you would use in the classroom?", you are testing their response for accuracy.

To test for skill, you generally have to ask participants to
demonstrate the skill. Asking how they would do something tells
you if they have the *knowledge* to do it, but it does not tell you if
they have the *skill* to do it. For example, participants may find it
an easy task to cite examples of how they would use open
questions in the classroom but be unable to actually do so once
they are in the classroom.

The best way to know if people have developed the skill to
do something is to watch them do it. If you want to know whether
participants have the skill to use open and closed questions
appropriately, give them an opportunity to make a presentation,
which allows them to demonstrate this skill. By observing their
performance, you will find out whether they have developed
adequate skills in this area.

Closed questions, while appropriate for conducting true and false tests, are inappropriate for other tests of knowledge. Asking participants "Do you understand?" (a common closed question) is a lousy way to test knowledge. All it tells you is whether participants think they understand. The open-ended question "What is your understanding?" is a much better question because the response will tell you whether participants have the understanding you want them to have. Generally, you do not need to ask every participant the same question to test for knowledge unless it is critical that each and every participant possess that knowledge. By randomly selecting participants and noting their responses, you can develop a pretty good idea of whether participants are picking up the knowledge intended.

Performance Standard 43: Instructor consistently provides correct and concise answers to questions asked by participants.

Simply stated, this standard says you are expected to answer questions accurately and concisely; don't make stuff up or elaborate unnecessarily. For most instructors, this seems an easy enough standard to meet. There are some instructors, however, who act as if they know the answer to every question asked. I'm not sure what causes this behavior. Perhaps these instructors, once face-to-face with a class full of participants, actually think they know the answer. Perhaps they are afraid they will lose credibility if they can't answer all questions. Whatever the reason, answering questions without knowing the answer simply doesn't work. At some point, your deception will be discovered and you will lose credibility.

There are also some instructors who can't seem to answer questions concisely. Excellent salespeople know that they can actually lose a sale by "selling beyond the close"—that is, by continuing their pitch too long. Instructors should know that giving ten bits of information when one will do is selling beyond the close, and it can cause participants to cease paying attention to learning objectives.

The way to meet this standard is to answer all questions correctly and concisely. If you do not know the answer to a question, the correct response is "I don't know." When you don't know or can't recall the answer and it is likely that someone in the class does possess the knowledge to accurately answer the question, toss the question back to the group. You can say, "I don't know, who can answer that question?" or, "Who would like to answer that question?" I'll have more to say about handling questions you are unable to answer in the next standard.

Performance Standard 44: Instructor, when unable to answer questions asked, generally researches answers and reports results back to participants.

When you don't know the answer to a question, let participants know you will find out the answer and report back to them. Then do it. By meeting this standard, you will often exceed the expectations of participants. When you demonstrate a willingness to go out of your way, participants take notice. When that happens, your credibility goes up and so does the participants' desire to learn.

There are a couple of practical exceptions to this standard. One exception is when there is no time remaining to research an answer. Another is when the question is unimportant or bears absolutely no relationship to the class at hand. Even in these instances, however, it may be worth researching answers to the questions asked. There is no rule that says instructors can't write or call participants once they have completed a course to report the results of research into questions asked.

Performance Standard 45: Instructor generally answers questions nondefensively.

This is a difficult standard, because it seems more obvious than it really is. To answer questions nondefensively, the instructor must not attack or put down participants for any questions asked or comments made. It's true that even in the face of hostility, most instructors aren't blatantly defensive; on the other hand, neither are they totally nondefensive. What most instructors do is to assume a behavior that I call "sugarcoating."

Sugarcoating is covering up defensive or offensive behavior with smiles, sweet tones of voice, and patronizing words or facial expressions. Let me give you an example of the way instructors commonly respond to defensive questions, offensive statements, and hostile participants. Assume that you have just completed a lecture on a new means of managing employees. Loudly and in a tone of voice that communicates blatant hostility, a participant says, "That lecture was the biggest bunch of garbage I've ever heard and a complete waste of my time." How do you respond? Even at your worst, it is unlikely you would say, "If you open your stupid mouth one more time, you're going to have to leave" or, "If you'd shut up and pay attention for a few minutes, you just might find out how important this information is to you."

What is likely is that you will say something like "I know that it might seem as if this is a waste of time, but if you will just stick with it, you will find out how valuable this information is to you." It's likely that you will say that with a smile and in a sweet tone of voice. It is also likely that your manner will come across as patronizing. That's sugarcoating, and it is just as defensive or offensive as more blatant behavior. A nondefensive response to such a question would be to say something like "It sounds as if you really disliked this lecture; is there something specific about it that bothers you, or is it the whole subject?" or "I really don't want to waste your time; tell me why you feel so strongly."

There are two critical things to do to respond nondefensively. First you must recognize that there is possibly some truth in what the participant says, regardless of how poorly it was said. Then you must respond by getting at the specifics of why the person feels so hostile. Regardless of what hostile participants say, it is seldom that they have a problem with everything that's just been said. More than likely something you said pushed the wrong button. By getting at specifics, you can identify and subsequently do something about the problem at hand. Responding nondefensively is tricky because most human beings tend to react rather than act. Instinctively, they would rather lash out at the hostile participant than employ nondefensive responding skills. Yet most instructors would be astounded by the productive results they can attain by responding nondefensively.

When hostile acts are initiated by participants, it causes instantaneous tension that is felt by everyone in the room. Once this happens, the remaining participants become absolutely mute, their eyes riveted on the instructor. They want to know what the instructor will do before deciding on their own reaction. If the instructor puts the participant down (acts defensively), the rest of the group will side with the participant. If the instructor reacts nondefensively, all eyes will turn to the hostile participant. If the hostile participant continues to be hostile, the group will join forces with the instructor. If the participant responds reasonably and the issue eventually becomes resolved, everyone will experience the release of tension. Participants will conclude that the instructor has their best interests at heart, and a sense of euphoria will fill the room. This may sound somewhat corny, but resolving potential disasters in a way that maintains everyone's self-esteem is euphoric.

Performance Standard 46: Instructor occasionally refers questions back to participants.

This standard means that instructors, when asked questions, should occasionally refer them to participants. Let me cite some examples. Barbara asks, "What do you mean by this standard?" Rather than answer this question, the instructor decides to toss it to the group for an answer. The instructor asks, "Who would like to answer that question?", and Charles does so. Here's another example: Nick asks, "Why would you want to refer questions back to participants rather than answer them yourself? After all, that's one of the reasons the instructor is there in the first place." The instructor says, "That's an important question, Nick. Who can tell us why an instructor might want to refer questions back to participants?" Diane raises her hand and says, "Referring questions back to participants is a way to get people actively involved in the learning process." The instructor then reinforces the response by noting that abundant participation equals abundant learning.

There are numerous benefits to referring questions back to participants. In addition to increasing participation, it gives the instructor time to think or relax. It also provides added opportunities to test for knowledge and measure participants' progress. The realization of any of these benefits makes using this standard worthwhile. However, there are certain occasions when referring questions back to participants is inappropriate. Do not refer questions back to the group if you suspect anyone, including yourself, might end up looking foolish or if you're certain that no one would know the answer. Finally, do not refer questions back to participants if you feel that doing so is simply inappropriate.

Performance Standard 47: Instructor occasionally guides participants to reach answers themselves.

When appropriate, instructors are expected to help participants answer questions or reach conclusions themselves. Too often, participants ask questions when they already know or could easily figure out the answers, but because they haven't thought through either the questions or the answers, they simply do not realize what they are capable of doing. For example, Lloyd says to the instructor, "Would you repeat the ten performance standards on questioning techniques?" The instructor recognizes that Lloyd can probably list most, if not all, of the standards himself. Instead of answering the question, the in-structor says, "Why don't you tell me which of the ten you already know, Lloyd, and if there are any you can't recall, I'll add them to your list." Lloyd finds that he is able to recall all ten. Here's another example: Jim says, "Can you give me an example of guiding participants to reach answers themselves?" The instruc-tor responds by saying, "What's an example you can think of, Jim?" Jim says, "Well, I guess what you are doing right now is a good example." The instructor responds, "That is a good exam-ple." In both of these examples, the participants, having an-swered the questions themselves, have come to realize that they are more capable than they thought. This realization is of real value.

By guiding participants to answer questions themselves, instructors increase participation and create time for them-selves to clarify their thinking. They also gain another method of testing for knowledge. However, there are times when it is inappropriate to employ this standard; namely, when anyone would be embarrassed or made to look foolish.

Performance Standard 48: Instructor generally handles irrele-vant questions appropriately.

Irrelevant questions are those that do not pertain in any way to the issue at hand. For many instructors, irrelevant ques-tions represent enormous thorns in their sides. For others, these questions are simply a nuisance. Whichever kind of instructor you happen to be, relief is on the way. While you can't absolutely control irrelevant questions, you can learn to handle them effec-tively and often effortlessly.

There is one simple ground rule that I want you to follow: if it takes longer to explain why a question is irrelevant than it does to answer the question, answer the question. Let me de-scribe what I've seen take place in the classroom. An instructor was leading an exciting discussion on learning disabilities when one of the participants raised his hand and asked, "Will there be any homework tonight?" Startled by the irrelevance of the question, the instructor collected himself and explained to the participant that the question was irrelevant to the discussion at hand; that he would cover homework later; that if there was a problem, he would be more than glad to take some time after class to talk about it; and that he would appreciate it if the participant would hold off asking any further such questions. Now, there was nothing wrong with what the instructor said; the problem was that it took him almost three minutes to say it. As a result, the excitement of the discussion simply died. In fact, the instructor resumed the discussion by saying, "Let's see, where were we?"

I want to change the aforementioned scenario slightly. The same instructor is leading the same exciting discussion, and the same participant asks, "Will there be any homework tonight?" Without missing a beat, the instructor says no and continues with the discussion. The irrelevant question has been answered in less than two seconds, which is not enough time to disrupt the rhythm of the discussion. Ninety-nine percent of the time, such handling of irrelevant questions will put an end to them. (Those occasions when they do become a problem are covered in Chapter Six under performance standard 20 and in the appendix.)

Participants who ask questions that are irrelevant are generally seeking attention or recognition. Rather than responding to their undesired behavior, seek out their thoughts and respond to the behaviors they demonstrate that are desirable. For example, in the above scenario, when the instructor said there would be no homework, he could easily have added, "What are your thoughts on learning disabilities?" which would have further acknowledged the participant.

Irrelevant questions annoy participants as well as instructors. By knowing in advance how to handle these questions, you decrease the likelihood that they will become bigger problems or that participants will ask even more of them.

You have just completed your review of the ten performance standards on questioning techniques. By perfecting your questioning skills, you will help participants meet their classroom objectives.

10

Using Training Aids
to Enhance Learning

*Instructors will perform with excellence if
they use training aids effectively.*

This chapter defines the performance standards related to use of training aids. Training aids enhance learning because they require participants to use their senses (hearing, seeing, touch, and so on) and people learn through their senses. Flip charts, slides, overhead projections, and blackboards all require participants to use their sense of hearing, while braille and typewriters call upon a person's sense of touch. Other training aids, such as video, television, computers, and movies, tackle multiple senses (sight and sound).

Because different people favor different senses, appealing to multiple senses enhances learning. For example, it can be helpful to use visual training aids in combination with lectures and discussion, which address the sense of hearing. Examples of the use of training aids will be given in each of the following discussions of the training aid standards.

Performance Standard 49: Instructor generally uses training aids so that they add to the learning experience.

Training aids are developed to enhance instruction not detract from it. They are not intended as a replacement for the instructor; they are intended to help the instructor reach learners. In order to meet this standard, instructors must use these aids as enhancements to learning. I think you will understand why after you read through the following two scenarios.

Billy is a new instructor who was asked to present a thirty-minute lecture on the use of training aids. Being quite nervous about the lecture, he prepared an extensive outline. Frightened that he wouldn't remember all that wanted to say, he also prepared dozens of detailed flip charts, which he read to participants. The lecture was a bomb, and Billy had no idea why.

The problem with this scenario is that Billy used the flip charts in a way that detracted from, rather than enhanced, learning. The charts were so complete that there was no need for Billy. It would have been a better decision to use flip charts to highlight the points Billy wanted to make rather than to contain every word that Billy wanted to say. If your training aids are so complete that you don't need to say anything to get your points across, send the aids out in written form and save yourself the time and cost associated with stand-up instruction.

Julie is incredibly organized. She enjoys a reputation of being attentive to details and is known to put a lot of extra time into preparing the courses she instructs. Her efforts generally have a high payoff. Recently, Julie was given a new training assignment, one that relied heavily on the use of flip charts to get the message across. She was quite excited about the assignment because it would enable her to make use of her creativity, a skill she felt she didn't have a chance to demonstrate in the other courses she taught. She spent a great deal of time preparing her flip charts, using a wide variety of colors and numerous drawings to highlight her points. She thought the artwork was good enough to be put in a show, and it was. Unfortunately, it was too good. When Julie presented her lecture, using the flip charts, no one paid any attention to what she had to say. They were so captivated by the beauty of her drawings, the strong use of color, and the exquisite detail that they lost any message that might have been delivered.

The most effective way to enhance learning is to use

simple words and draw simple pictures. If your drawings are more effective than the message, participants are more likely to remember the drawings than they are the message. I've seen dozens of instructors successfully use stick figures to depict people and little boxes to represent buildings. I've seen instructors effectively use napkins, pencils, paper, swizzle sticks, balloons, jelly beans, doughnuts, costumes, and even a live donkey to enhance learning.

Performance Standard 50: Instructor generally demonstrates proficiency in using training aids.

There are a number of ground rules that can help make you proficient in using training aids. Below are listed the advantages and disadvantages of six commonly used training aids and specific tips for using each one.

Overhead Projectors

Overhead projectors are excellent training aids for many reasons. Because overhead projectors operate like a giant magnifying glass, they make it easy for all participants, including large groups of people, to see what has been written. The projectors are simple to use, require little maintenance, and can be used with the lights on. The transparencies (the film used with the equipment) can be written or drawn on and can be prepared in advance or made up during class, whichever is most desirable. The transparencies are relatively inexpensive to buy and, because of their size (8 ½ × 11 inches), can easily be transported. In addition, the equipment is commonly available and relatively inexpensive to rent. Because of their many advantages, overhead projectors are one of the most popular training aids used today. However, they are not without disadvantages.

The transparencies used with the overhead projectors are slippery, especially those that have not been framed. I once let fifty of them slip out of my hand during a lecture; it took fifteen minutes to pick them up and put them back in order. Overhead projectors are not as flexible as some training aids, such as flip charts. Because the transparencies are so small, there is not much room for writing or drawing on them. Because the projector is a piece of equipment, it is subject to equipment problems, the most common of which is a dead bulb.

Because the advantages far outweigh the disadvantages, however, the overhead projector has become a training staple. You can demonstrate proficiency in using this training aid by adhering to the following ground rules:

1. Write big. Making your letters two to three times bigger than typewriter size will enable everyone to see what you have written.
2. Put no more than seven lines on the transparency and spread those lines evenly across the transparency. This, combined with large writing, will ensure legibility.
3. Frame your transparencies with cardboard or plastic frames, even if you are using blank transparencies. This reduces the likelihood that they will slip out of your hand.
4. Number your transparencies. This makes it easy to keep them in order.
5. Keep a spare projector bulb handy and know how to install it.
6. Practice using the overhead projector before class begins, and position it so everyone can see it.
7. Turn the projector off when you are not using it. If you leave the equipment on, the bright screen will distract participants from the task at hand.

Slide Projectors

Slide projectors have many advantages as a training aid. Unlike most other training aids, slide projectors can produce visually stunning images, including beautiful photography and wonderful graphics. Yet slide projectors are easy to operate, and, because they greatly magnify images, they make it easy for participants to see what's going on. Slide projectors are generally available and easy to rent. The slides themselves are compact and easy to transport.

Unlike the overhead projector, the disadvantages of the slide projector often outweigh its advantages. The slides must be prepared in advance, and once they are prepared, the instructor has little flexibility in using them. Slides can't be written on, nor can they easily be changed. Slides are most effective shown in a darkened room, which requires turning lights on and off, making it almost impossible to see the faces and judge the reactions of participants. A darkened room can encourage participants to nod off and can make it difficult for them to take notes. Like overhead transparencies, the slides themselves can be slippery. The equipment is often more sophisticated than most overhead projectors and consequently has more parts that can break down.

Nonetheless, there will still be times when a slide projector is the most effective training aid to use. The ground rules for using the slide projector are similar to those for using the overhead projector:

1.   Write big.
2.   Use seven or fewer lines, spread evenly across the slide.
3.   Frame your slides.
4.   Number your slides.
5.   Keep a spare bulb and know how to install it.
6.   Practice using the equipment before you actually begin class, and position it so everyone can see the projected image.
7.   Turn off the machine when you are not using it.
8.   To discourage nodding off, show slides primarily in the mornings, occasionally in the afternoons, and never right after lunch.

Movie Projectors

With the increased popularity of video, movie projectors are being seen less and less in the classroom. Nevertheless, the movie projector is an excellent training aid, especially in large classes where a big screen may be preferable to several video monitors. There also may be occasions when the impact of the message is such that only the big screen of the movies will do.

Movie projectors have lost some of their appeal as training aids because video equipment is generally more cost-effective, more easily available, and easier to operate and maintain. When something goes wrong with a movie projector, few instructors are able to repair it. Movie films are also rather expensive and bulky, which makes transportation awkward. In addition, they possess the same disadvantages as slides in that they can't be altered and they must be shown in darkened rooms.

There are three ground rules to follow when using movie projectors:

1. Practice using the equipment before class begins.
2. Keep a spare projector bulb handy and know how to install it.
3. Show movies primarily in the mornings, occasionally in the afternoons, and never right after lunch.

Video Equipment

The advent of video has made a tremendous impact on classroom training. With a video camera and playback unit, instructors can easily tape participants in action and then play back the recorded tapes. There is no better method than this for providing participants with instant feedback. Video equipment is also effective for showing short video vignettes (such as examples of desired behavior) and complete movies. Unlike movie and slide projectors, they can be used effectively in normal light. Video-tapes are inexpensive and, because of their size, easy to transport. Because of the enormous popularity of home video units, most everyone is adept at operating the equipment as well as fixing minor problems or making minor adjustments. Video equipment generally requires minimal maintenance.

There are a few disadvantages to video equipment. You can't write on it. The cost of complete units is expensive, and the units are not easily transported. Because of the small screen, video can exaggerate movements or expressions. Minor flaws, like a facial tic or a shaky hand, seem more pronounced than they really are. This can make it difficult to use video successfully as a feedback tool.

The ground rules for using video are simple:

1. Set up the equipment and practice using it before class starts.
2. If you plan to record, have extra blank videotapes available in case any of the tapes are damaged.
3. Before taping, ask participants to write their names and the beginning counter numbers on each tape. This will help prevent recording over valuable material and make it easy to find the start of taped segments.
4. Before recording, check that participants did not rewind their tapes (this also helps prevent taping over valuable material).
5. After recording, note the ending counter number on the tape.
6. Use video any time of the day; however, avoid showing movies after lunch or at the end of the day.

Tape Recorders

Tape recorders are excellent training aids. They are compact; consequently, they are easy to transport. They are also easy to use and maintain. They are excellent tools for recording training exercises. When used to let participants listen to themselves, tape recorders are an excellent source of feedback. They are also immensely helpful when used to practice a presentation or prepare a talk. Tapes are inexpensive and readily available. They are also excellent for listening to a lecture, a speech, a story, or music.

There are a few drawbacks to the tape recorder. It's possible to erase or record over your tape. In addition, tapes eventually wear out, and they occasionally break. However, these occurrences are generally nothing more than minor irritations because replacement tapes are cheap and easily available. The greatest drawback to the tape recorder is that it is less versatile than other training aids.

The ground rules for using tape recorders are basically the same as those for using videotape recorders:

1. Practice using tape recorders prior to the start of class.
2. If you plan to record, have extra blank tapes available.
3. Before recording, ask participants to write their names and the beginning counter numbers on their tapes.
4. Before recording, check that participants did not rewind their tapes.
5. After recording, note ending counter numbers on the tapes.
6. Use tape recorders at any time.

Flip Charts

Without a doubt, the flip chart is my favorite training aid. It has great flexibility, and it can be prepared in advance or used spontaneously. It is easy to use, easy to see, relatively easy to transport, and inexpensive. It is an excellent device to help instructors recall important points. By lightly penciling notes on the flip chart in advance, the instructor can easily recall important points. It will appear to participants as if the instructor is speaking from memory rather than from notes (the penciled notes are invisible to participants), which will do much to build the instructor's confidence.

Flip charts are easy to use and can be just as easily used by participants as by instructors. If you make a mistake in using the flip chart, all you have to do is tear off the paper, throw it away, and start over again. In addition, flip charts can be easily saved and easily displayed. By tearing off the sheets of paper and posting them with masking tape, you can display dozens of them around the room for all participants to see. This is invaluable when it is important for participants to refer to the information the charts contain. There is very little that can go wrong with a flip chart. Occasionally, you might find a wobbly leg on the easel, and it's possible for an easel to be knocked over or broken, but these occasions are so rare that it is safe to call the device foolproof.

There are few disadvantages to the flip chart as a training aid. It is not effective in large rooms with hundreds of participants—it's simply too small to be easily seen by that many people. When positioned poorly, it's difficult for all participants to see without craning their necks. Some of the felt-tip pens used with the flip charts smell funny and can dry out quickly if their caps are left off. That's about it for the disadvantages of this excellent training aid.

There are quite a few ground rules for using this aid effectively:

1. Determine, in advance, the number of flip charts you want to use. I generally use two for myself and one for each participant group, as appropriate.
2. Set the flip charts in positions where all participants can easily see them. Prior to the start of class sit in participants' chairs to ensure that all participants will be able to see the flip charts.
3. Lightly pencil in points you want to recall on blank sheets.
4. When preparing easels in advance, use masking tape to number or code each sheet of paper. For example, fold the masking tape over the side of the paper, letting an inch or so show, and code or number the tapes. This will enable you to easily find your prepared sheets when you are instructing in the classroom.
5. Keep an extra pad of paper available at all times.
6. Keep extra felt-tip pens available.
7. When using the flip chart, try not to turn your back to participants; write from the side of the flip chart rather than facing it (this is a skill that will come with practice).
8. Write big.
9. Write no more than seven lines on a sheet.
10. Don't worry about being an artist or a spelling bee champion. You won't be judged by your art or perfect spelling. Rough sketches, abbreviations, and even the occasional misspelled word will help you make your points. Here is a

good rule of thumb: if finding out how to accurately spell a word interferes with the learning taking place, go ahead and misspell it.

There are many other training aids that instructors use— blackboards, story boards, computers, and so forth. Most of the ground rules listed in this chapter can be applied to other training aids. Regardless of what training aids you use, you can read through the tips presented here to come up with your own set of ground rules for each one.

Performance Standard 51: Instructor generally performs minor maintenance or adjustments on training aids, as required.

Instructors are expected to perform minor maintenance on training aids, such as changing projector bulbs, cleaning the camera lens, adjusting horizontal and vertical holds on television monitors, and so forth. Instructors are not expected to repair a broken movie projector or fix a damaged tape head, but by knowing how to carry out minor maintenance and adjustments, they can avoid major headaches. Generally the instruction booklets that come with most training aids provide troubleshooting guidelines that can be useful in this respect. Instructors should have access to resources for repairing broken equipment.

Performance Standard 52: Instructor generally uses alternative training aids, as necessary.

This standard simply says to use alternative training aids when problems arise that prevent you from using the training aid you planned to use. This is another standard designed to eliminate potential problems.

If your overhead equipment breaks down, switching to the flip chart is usually easy and effective. If you run out of flip chart paper, a blackboard or even cardboard can be an adequate alternative. I've used 8½ × 11–inch pieces of paper to make miniature flip charts and paper napkins to serve as replacements for 8½ × 11–inch pieces of paper. It's a good idea to think ahead of time about possible problems you might encounter with training aids. By having an idea what you would do in the event of a problem, you increase the likelihood that you will successfully resolve it.

Performance Standard 53: Instructor consistently follows specified safety practices in using training aids.

This is one of those standards where I want to use the word *always* in place of *consistently*, even though I know that using the word *always* doesn't always produce the results I desire. Consequently, I expect instructors to consistently (rather than always) follow specified safety practices in using training aids. In the absence of such information (which is commonly available in the instruction booklets that accompany training aids and equipment), instructors are to use common sense. The most common accident in the classroom is tripping over a cord. An easy way to prevent such an accident is to tape the cord to the floor or carpet.

Instructors are also expected to be familiar with emergency procedures and exits. They should know where first aid equipment and supplies are kept and be sure that these items are maintained. Although not required, it's a good idea to know standard first-aid measures.

Performance Standard 54: Instructor consistently follows prescribed instructions in caring for training aids.

This performance standard is rather obvious. It asks that you take care when using and storing training aids and equipment. It is similar to performance standard 53 in that you are expected to follow the instructions detailed in the booklets that generally accompany training aids and to use common sense in handling those aids. For example, most equipment (video and tape recorders, cameras, slide projectors, and so on) requires some cleaning and maintenance. When not in use, these items should be carefully stored and protected from dust, heat, cold, and other harm. Basically, instructors are expected to treat training aids and equipment just as they would personal equipment they value.

You have just completed the fifth set of performance standards developed to help you become a successful instructor. We will turn now to the performance standards that pertain to evaluating instruction.

11

Collecting and Making Sense of Evaluation Data

Instructors will perform with excellence if they use evaluation data capably.

This chapter defines the performance standards that let instructors know what kinds of evaluations they are expected to do. Excellent instructors know that by evaluating the performance of participants they can help participants meet training objectives and contribute to strengthening the course. By assessing their own performance, they can develop their skills in the classroom.

Of the six performance standards discussed here, the first two deal with the evaluation of participant performance and are intended to help participants meet course objectives. The next two relate to the evaluation of course content and are designed to ensure that all material is current and of high quality. The final two relate to instructor performance and are intended to help instructors strengthen their own performance.

Performance Standard 55: Instructor consistently evaluates participant performance, as appropriate.

This standard asks you to collect feedback so that you know how participants are progressing toward the attainment of course objectives. This standard can be partially met by meeting performance standard 42 (using questions to test participants) and by administering the quizzes, tests, and exercises that are often a part of course material.

You might recall from Chapter Nine the many ways you can test for knowledge, skills, and attitudes. For example, asking open questions is an excellent way to evaluate the knowledge of participants. Asking participants to summarize lessons or key points and asking them how they would apply the principle being taught are also good methods to evaluate participants.

Observing performance is the best means of judging whether participants have developed the skills required to move ahead. For example, assume that one course objective is to train participants to use a new method of providing feedback to employees. A role-playing exercise would be an excellent vehicle to measure participant performance because it enables you to observe participants providing feedback and gives you data that tells you whether participants have developed the skills to move ahead.

Quizzes and tests are the most effective ways of judging whether participants have developed required knowledge. They are usually built into course material; if they are not, you can develop your own quizzes and tests by referring to a good book on the subject, such as Robert F. Mager's *Making Instruction Work*.

Performance Standard 56: Instructor consistently provides feedback to participants, as required.

There are two kinds of feedback to use in the classroom. The first kind reinforces good performance — it is feedback that acknowledges people for doing what you want them to do. For example, if a group of participants have successfully completed a role-playing exercise, it is appropriate to reinforce their performance by thanking them and telling them how the behaviors they exhibited met your expectations. This kind of feedback is called *motivational feedback*.

The second kind of feedback is called *developmental feedback*, and it is intended to help participants develop or correct their performance. For example, if the participants were unsuccessful in the exercise described above, it would be appropriate for the instructor to let participants know what they should do differently. Motivational and developmental feedback require instructors to become classroom coaches rather than classroom judges. Both forms of feedback, when used appropriately, contribute to participants meeting course objectives. You will learn more about these feedback concepts in Chapter Twelve.

Performance Standard 57: Instructor consistently reviews course feedback on all evaluations and takes appropriate action.

Basically, this standard says that instructors are expected to review all feedback, including daily, end-of-course, and follow-up evaluations, and determine what action to take to improve the course. Let's look at three scenarios focusing on different types of feedback.

In the first scenario, Marty is instructing a three-day program in presentation skills. The feedback he receives at the end of the first day suggests that the pace was a bit too slow and the room a little too hot for several of the participants. In addition, two participants asked if it would be possible to shorten the lunch break on the third day so that they could keep an important commitment. Marty begins the second day by checking and subsequently lowering the room temperature. Prior to class he reviews the pacing of the day and decides to shorten a couple of lectures. He also decides to poll participants with respect to shortening lunch on the third day. He plans to review the daily feedback sheets from the previous day with participants and to let them know what actions he will take as a result of the feedback.

In the second scenario, Janet has just completed the first of four one-day management skills programs. Puzzled by the fact that four participants rated the program as too long, four rated it as too short, and four rated it as just right, she isn't sure what to do with the feedback. Consequently, she decides to ask the next group of participants to elaborate on their responses to the question concerning course length.

In the third scenario, Mark reviewed a set of follow-up evaluations that were turned in six months after the completion of a series of management seminars. Eight of the nine training objectives were rated as useful; the ninth was rated as not useful by over 40 percent of the managers who completed evaluations. Mark decided to conduct a group of interviews to test the validity of the feedback and discovered that the ninth objective was no longer required due to changes in the managers' jobs. As a result, he was able to save time and money by eliminating the ninth objective from the course. In all three scenarios, the instructors dutifully reviewed the course evaluations and took appropriate action.

There are three good ways to collect this kind of feedback: testing, observing, and data gathering. Testing is an ideal tool for measuring knowledge, as observation is for measuring skills, and data gathering for collecting opinions. Most evaluations fall into the third category, which is one reason evaluations are so often referred to as "smile tests"—that is, tests that determine little more than how much the instructor smiled at participants. An entertaining instructor, for example, will generally enjoy high evaluation marks regardless of whether participants meet course objectives. Frankly, I feel there is nothing wrong with "smile tests," for they do collect participants' opinions, and that is information instructors need to help participants meet training objectives. However, smile tests are seldom sufficient. To collect factual evidence, you must test (to measure knowledge) and observe (to measure skills). Let's take a close look at daily, end-of-course, and follow-up evaluations.

Daily Evaluations

The purpose of the daily evaluation is to gain feedback that you can use immediately to reinforce, develop, or correct performance. It should be simple, easy to complete, quick to do, and (like all evaluations) anonymous. I use a variation of the following list of questions for every course I teach because it gives me a sense of how participants view the overall program, what they liked, and what they believe can be done immediately to improve the program. It also gives them an opportunity to comment on other areas.

1. On a 1 (low) to 10 (high) scale, how would you rate the overall value of the day?
2. What did you like best about the day?
3. What would make tomorrow's session even better?
4. What additional comments would you like to make?

I like to feed the results of daily evaluations back to participants as it encourages them to take responsibility for the results. I report the results of questions one, two, and (if appropriate) four at the end of the day and question three at the beginning of the next day, when it is immediately useful. This simple form of feedback can be used as is for most training programs.

End-of-Course Evaluations

The purpose of end-of-course evaluations is to collect data that will be useful the next time you conduct the program. It also provides input to those responsible for course revisions. Like the daily evaluation, the end-of-course evaluation should be simple, easy to complete, quick to do, and anonymous. The main difference between these two forms of evaluation is that the end-of-course evaluation collects more detailed information and specifically addresses course objectives. Exhibit 11.1 is an actual end-of-course evaluation from a management program on selection.

Exhibit 11.1. End-of-Course Evaluation.

Course: Selection

Date: _____

Instructor: _____

Please answer the following questions by circling your response and providing comments where appropriate.

1. Overall, how would you rate the value of this program?

1	2	3	4	5	6	7	8	9	10
Not valuable at all			Somewhat valuable			Valuable			Very valuable

2. Overall, how effective was this session at building your skills in:

   a. Preparing for an interview?

1	2	3	4	5	6	7	8	9	10
Not effective at all			Somewhat effective			Effective			Very effective

   b. Conducting the interview?

1	2	3	4	5	6	7	8	9	10
Not effective at all			Somewhat effective			Effective			Very effective

   c. Making the selection decision?

1	2	3	4	5	6	7	8	9	10
Not effective at all			Somewhat effective			Effective			Very effective

3. How appropriate was the length of the program?

1	2	3	4	5	6	7	8	9	10
Too short				Perfect				Too long	

4. How appropriate was the pacing of the program?

1	2	3	4	5	6	7	8	9	10
Too slow				Perfect				Too fast	

Exhibit 11.1. End-of-Course Evaluation, Cont'd.

---

5. What was your overall interest level?

    1   2   3   4   5   6   7   8   9   10
       Little   Some   Interested   High
       or no   interest   interest
       interest

6. How would you rate the usefulness of the tools provided?

    1   2   3   4   5   6   7   8   9   10
       Not   Somewhat   Useful   Very
       useful   useful   useful

7. What specifically did you like about the program?

    _____

    _____

    _____

8. What did you like about the instructor's performance?

    _____

    _____

    _____

9. What would make this a better program?

    _____

    _____

10. What would improve the instructor's performance?

    _____

    _____

Review end-of-course evaluations immediately following the completion of the program, focusing your attention on questions one through eight. This is also the time to forward relevant data to those responsible for course updates or revisions. When you prepare to teach your next training session, you should focus on questions nine and ten, because only then is the information immediately useful. By adapting questions two and six to fit your subject matter, you can use this evaluation or a variation of it for most training programs.

Follow-Up Evaluation

The basic purpose of the follow-up evaluation is to collect information that will be useful in conducting future courses. The follow-up evaluation identifies if and how well trainees have applied the training skills to their jobs. There are a number of ways to collect this data. The most effective is to observe participants on the job and measure their performance against the objectives of the training. Another is to ask their supervisors to do the same thing. The third is to use a post-course questionnaire to collect participants' perceptions of their ability to apply what they have learned. Exhibit 11.2 provides a sample of such a questionnaire.

You should review the follow-up data you collect immediately before you teach the course again because that is when the

Exhibit 11.2. Follow-Up Evaluation.

1. Recently, you attended a training program on (state subject). For each objective listed, note whether you have applied what you learned on your job and rate how effectively you applied your learning on a 1 (low) to 10 (high) scale.

Objective	Applied to Job?	Effectiveness
(List objectives here)	(Yes/No)	(Rate 1 to 10)

2. Overall, how would you rate the value of the program?

1	2	3	4	5	6	7	8	9	10
Not valuable			Somewhat valuable			Valuable			Very valuable

3. How has the program affected the way you do your job?

4. What specifically did you like about the program?

5. What would make the program better?

6. What did you like about the instructor's performance?

7. What would improve the instructor's performance?

8. What other comments would you like to make?

information will be most useful to you. In addition, you should forward the data you collect to those responsible for making course revisions.

Performance Standard 58: Instructor consistently refers items likely to require action to the appropriate group or individual.

This standard simply says that instructors are expected to refer all items requiring action to the individual or group responsible for acting on the item. For example, many organizations have course development groups. In these organizations, the course development group is the appropriate place to refer recommended revisions in course content, course development ideas, and so forth. Simple updating is usually carried out by the instructor.

In organizations without course developers, instructors are often responsible for developing course material. In some organizations, however, responsibility for course development and revision lies with an outside organization, and it is to this group that the instructor should refer recommended changes. By referring items requiring action to the appropriate individual or group, you ensure that these items are given the expert attention they deserve.

Performance Standard 59: Instructor consistently reviews feedback to instructor and takes appropriate action.

One of the wonderful things about being an instructor is that you actually receive feedback on a regular basis. What this performance standard says is that you are expected to review all such feedback and take appropriate action on it. For example, I recall receiving feedback on a train-the-trainer program I conducted that said my lectures were too long. After some thought, I decided not to shorten the lectures; instead, I decided to increase the frequency with which I used participants to bring out the key points. As a result, the feedback at the end of the next session was positive about both using participants and delivering lectures.

End-of-course evaluations are a part of most training programs, and they usually include a section related to instructor performance. This feedback often comes too late. That's why I also recommend that instructors collect feedback daily. By simply asking participants to identify the instructor behaviors that they liked, would like to see more of, or would like to see less of, you can collect feedback you can use the following day. By knowing at the end of the first day of a five-day course that the pacing is off, the instructor can take immediate action to improve the remaining four days. If you wait until the end of the course, you can't take any action until the next time you teach the course.

The advantage that end-of-course and follow-up feedback have over daily feedback is that the comments are often more detailed and, as a result, more useful. With end-of-course and follow-up feedback, the time to focus attention on making improvements is the next time you prepare to teach the course. Some instructors tend to fret about end-of-course feedback when they receive it. This is a waste of time and energy since there is little instructors can do to change their behavior until the next time they teach. If you receive end-of-course or follow-up feedback that indicates areas in which you can improve your performance, put it in your file until the next time you are preparing to teach.

Performance Standard 60: Instructor consistently evaluates own performance and takes appropriate action.

Instructors can assess their own performance using the assessment tool discussed in Chapter Twelve. This tool is a

shortened version of the sixty performance standards for instructors. It has been designed as a checklist so that instructors
can use the tool to evaluate their performance. This performance standard asks you to complete the checklist at the end of
each training program and identify those standards of performance you met, exceeded, or fell short of meeting. This information can be invaluable to your development as an excellent
instructor.

I want to suggest that you use the instructor assessment
tool of the next chapter (Exhibit 12.1) in the following way.
Circle M next to those standards you met and circle E next to
those you exceeded. If a particular standard did not apply, write
NA in the comments column. If you fell short of meeting a
particular standard, circle NM in the results column and make a
note next to the standard of what occurred. Now focus your
attention on those standards that you met or exceeded. Simply
ignore those standards you fell short of meeting. The time to
address those items is when you are next preparing to teach. By
congratulating yourself for what you did accomplish and not
punishing yourself for what you didn't, you increase the likelihood that you will execute all sixty performance standards
successfully.

You have just reviewed the final set of performance standards for instructors. Because these standards are the backbone
of the instructor job, it is important for you to have some way of
knowing if you are meeting them. In the next chapter we will
turn to an assessment tool that can be used by both instructors
and their supervisors to determine if instructors are doing an
effective job.

PART THREE

Managing Instructor Excellence

12

Observing Instructors and Providing Feedback

Instructors will perform with excellence if they receive feedback that reinforces and develops excellent performance.

T his chapter discusses motivational and developmental feedback in more depth and links the instructor performance standards to an effective instructor feedback system. If you manage instructors, this chapter will enable you to provide feedback to instructors that will reinforce excellent performance (motivational feedback) and develop performance that can be strengthened (developmental feedback). It will also provide you with tools to document instructor performance, conduct progress reviews, handle difficult performance discussions, and complete performance appraisals, which are the formal feedback mechanisms of most organizations. If you are an instructor, this chapter will help you assess and strengthen your own performance.

Most instructors work in organizations where feedback does not reinforce or develop excellent performance. Like many other supervisors, training managers have a tendency to ignore feedback, especially feedback that reinforces good perfor-

mance. Many believe that if people are doing a good job, they
don't need to be told so. Others believe that the nature of the
instructor's job makes it impossible to provide adequate feedback. However, instructors who do not receive feedback on their
performance are likely to conclude that their performance in
the classroom simply does not matter, and their classroom
performance is likely to deteriorate as a result.

Like most supervisors, training managers think of feedback as either positive or negative. While positive feedback
clearly reinforces positive performance, negative feedback just
as clearly reinforces negative performance. Thinking of feedback in terms of negative and positive does not develop excellent instructor performance. In addition, when managers give
feedback, they often send messages that accomplish the exact
opposite of what they intended because the messages are either
ill timed or ill conceived. The end result is that feedback to
instructors is generally useless.

Criteria for Excellent Feedback

Excellent feedback meets the following criteria:

1. Motivational and developmental feedback are used to rein-
    force and develop excellent performance.
2. Motivational and developmental feedback are given
    separately.
3. Motivational feedback is given immediately following per-
    formance; developmental feedback is given *as close as possible*
    to the next time the performance will be repeated.
4. Feedback is described in terms of what you observed and is
    related to the instructor performance standards.
5. Motivational feedback is given either privately or publicly;
    developmental feedback is only given privately.
6. Feedback is given sincerely.

Some of these criteria require a significant change of
thinking on the part of most managers. For example, you will be
required to shift your thinking from familiar concepts (positive

and negative feedback) to unfamiliar concepts (motivational and developmental feedback). Some criteria call for actions that are the exact opposite of what you have probably been trained to do—for example, separating different kinds of feedback. Let us look at each of these criteria more closely.

Motivational and Developmental Feedback

Most managers are uncomfortable giving employees negative feedback and with good reason. It doesn't work, and it throws the manager into the role of judge, for which most managers are ill equipped. Some managers promote the use of so-called constructive criticism, but this doesn't solve the problem. Frankly, there is nothing constructive about criticism. What is needed is a completely different approach.

Donald Tosti, founding partner of the Vanguard Consulting Group (San Rafael, California) and an acknowledged expert in the area of feedback, transformed thinking about feedback with his work on summative and formative feedback, also known as motivational and developmental feedback (Tosti, 1986). Motivational (summative) feedback is akin to positive feedback. Its purpose is to reinforce performance that meets or exceeds expectations. For instance: "That was a clear example you used to demonstrate the concept of setting performance expectations. I liked that you tied the example to each of the steps involved in the process. It made it easy for the participants to follow, and it clearly met what I expected of you." Another example: "You handled that question about career development very nicely. It was a difficult question, and the facts you had at your fingertips and the concise way you presented them exceeded what I expected. It was very nicely done." We have all seen good examples of motivational feedback.

Developmental (formative) feedback is intended to strengthen performance, including performance that falls short of expectations. (It is not intended to resolve difficult performance problems, however—a topic that is covered later in this chapter.) The following three examples show the difference between negative and developmental feedback.

Negative Feedback	*Developmental Feedback*
"That was really a lousy presentation you made. I'm surprised the vice president didn't throw us out of the staff meeting."	"I think that your next presentation to the vice president will be greatly strengthened by having a clear and concise objective. I'd like to review your plans for the next presentation."
"Last month's financial report was incomplete and not very useful."	"Last month's financial report was missing summary data. I think next month's report will be much better with such data included."
"I guess it wasn't all that bad, considering it was your first time in the classroom. When you started to read from the leader's guide, I thought everyone would fall asleep. On top of that, you looked very uncomfortable."	"The next time you conduct this session, I would like you to use your leader's guide as a guide rather than a script. I think that will make a big difference in terms of your comfort level and your performance."

Developmental feedback requires that training managers look for ways to help instructors improve their performance. This takes managers out of the role of judge and puts them into the role of coach, which is much more likely to produce desired results. Imagine how impossible it would be for any sporting team to play effectively if the role of the coach was merely to point out what was wrong. Excellent coaches know that their role is to help team members play at their optimum level of performance. Negative feedback has no such inherent concept of "helping" and, as such, possesses little power to improve performance.

Separating Motivational and Developmental Feedback

If you're like most managers, you were trained to mix feedback messages. In other words, you were taught that when you had something negative to say, you should sandwich it in between two pieces of positive feedback. Unfortunately, this sandwiching leaves performers confused about the message being communicated. While many managers have abandoned this technique as ineffective, others continue to practice it because it is the only thing they know how to do.

An important reason for not mixing feedback is that when given a combination of positive and negative feedback, people have a propensity to focus on one or the other. Most tend to focus on the negative and discount the positive, even though the amount of negative feedback may be minuscule compared to the positive. A small proportion of people hear only the positive, turning a deaf ear to the negative. If you have ten things to communicate and one of them is even the slightest bit negative, this type of person will hear only the nine positive things.

Timing of Feedback

Motivational feedback should be given immediately after the performance is observed and developmental feedback just prior to the next time the performance takes place. Much of the feedback managers do give subordinates is useless because of poor timing. For example, it is relatively ineffective to tell an employee what he or she could have done to improve a presentation when there won't be another presentation for months. By the time the next presentation rolls around, the employee will have forgotten the ideas for improvement. It's just as ineffective to tell an employee that the presentation he or she gave two months ago was nicely done. The employee is left wondering why it took you so long to give the feedback and usually will conclude (because of the time lapse) that it couldn't be very important.

The timing of both motivational and developmental feedback is important to reinforcing performance. By giving motivational feedback at the end of a task, you make the employee aware of those things that contributed to its success. This is an excellent way to ensure that the performance is repeated. By giving developmental feedback just prior to a performance, you increase the likelihood that the performance will be successful. Let's look at an example.

Mark has just completed a three-day technical skills program. You observed the closing segment of the class. You noted that he succinctly and accurately summarized the main concepts of the program, demonstrated excellent use of training aids, and gave clear and concise instructions on completing the post-course evaluation. You also noted that he tended to focus his eye contact on participants in the back of the room and to his right, ignoring people on his immediate left.

Immediately following class, you sit down with Mark and go over the things he did well. You note that Mark will be instructing another class the following week. You make arrangements to meet with him at the beginning of his preparation time, prior to the start of the session. At this meeting you tell Mark that you believe his performance will be enhanced if he focuses his eye contact on all parts of the room, especially the left-hand side, which he tended to ignore the last time you observed his performance. This information will enable Mark to immediately improve his performance. If you happen to observe this class and note that he includes the left-hand side of the room in his eye contact, you get to give him motivational feedback to that effect.

The above example is ideal; practically, it may not be possible for you to meet with Mark a second time. When this happens, it is still important to separate the two kinds of feedback. First give Mark the same motivational feedback you gave in the above example and ask if he has any questions about it. Then tell him that because you won't be able to meet with him prior to his next course, you would also like to give him some developmental feedback. Check to see that he understands and then let him know he can improve his performance if he focuses on all sides of the room.

Specificity of Feedback

Many training managers give feedback in such general terms that the feedback is virtually meaningless to instructors. Common remarks such as "nice job," "excellent," "not bad," and the like leave too much room for interpretation. Compare such remarks to the following examples:

- "Writing big, as you did on the easel, made it very easy for all participants to see what you were writing. That is exactly what I was hoping to see."
- "The lesson you presented on handling difficult performance problems was absolutely on target. The steps you covered were useful, and the number and quality of examples you used clearly exceeded what I expected."
- "You fell short of expectations when you asked John to leave because he was so disruptive. There are three or four additional steps you can take to defuse situations like this one. I would like to go over them with you because I think it will help you the next time you're faced with a similar situation."

Each of the above examples describes what you observed and lets the instructors know what specific standards they have met, exceeded, or failed to meet.

Private and Public Feedback

Motivational feedback can be given both privately and publicly. The only exception is if public feedback would severely embarrass the instructor. Public feedback is intended to reinforce private feedback rather than substitute for it. Used appropriately, it is a very nice way of providing recognition and reinforcing desired behavior.

It is inappropriate, and often disastrous, to give developmental feedback in front of others. It can be embarrassing to receive such feedback publicly, and it does nothing to develop the desired performance of the instructor. Give developmental feedback in private.

Sincerity of Feedback

Be sincere when giving feedback; instructors are quick to pick up insincerity in communications. When feedback sounds insincere, it is usually quickly discounted by the instructor. By exhibiting a genuine desire to let people know how well they are doing and by sincerely working to develop an instructor's performance in the classroom, you are practicing excellent feedback. Your behavior will be noticed and appreciated by your employees.

Both motivational and developmental feedback will do precisely what they are intended to do if you adhere to the six criteria discussed above. Motivational feedback will reinforce excellent performance, and developmental feedback will develop excellent performance. While neither will solve serious performance problems, they will enable you to increase your comfort and skill levels in this sometimes difficult area of job performance.

Observing Instructor Performance

It is shocking to discover the number of training managers who do not observe instructor performance. There is no way to know whether an instructor is meeting, exceeding, or falling short of performance standards unless you observe the instructor's performance. End-of-course evaluations won't give you that information, nor will participants' testimony, nor will a videotape showing the instructor in the classroom. The only accurate and fair way is to observe performance.

New instructors should be observed weekly until they demonstrate the ability to consistently meet performance standards, and then monthly thereafter. Instructors with a year or more of experience should be observed monthly or quarterly, depending upon their level of skill and the results of previous observations. Instructors with serious performance problems (those who frequently do not meet performance standards) should be observed weekly or even daily until the performance problems are successfully eliminated.

Observing should not be an unpleasant experience for instructors, observers, or participants. The best way to set up observations is for instructors to announce at the beginning of class that they have invited their training manager to come in and observe a portion of the session. They should explain that the purpose of the observation is to help the instructor develop training skills and that the observation has no purpose relative to participants, so hopefully participants will relax despite the slight intrusion.

Observers should recognize that they are an intrusion, however slight; consequently, they should quietly take a seat and should not participate except in extreme emergencies. Training managers should take care not to ignore this advice. If managers participate in training sessions, they can endanger the credibility given instructors by participants. They also seriously risk losing whatever trust the instructor places in them.

The instructor assessment tool in Exhibit 12.1 provides training managers with a means to document instructor performance. You will note that this tool is a condensed version of the instructor performance standards, which can also be used by instructors to assess their own classroom performance.

The following guidelines should help you successfully carry out observation of instructors.

1. Prior to the observation, go over previous instructor observations to identify performance standards in need of review.
2. Select a segment of the program that will enable you to observe a number of these areas.
3. Select a time to provide motivational feedback.
4. Notify the instructor of the segment you will observe (optional) and the time selected for giving the motivational feedback.
5. On the day of the observation, enter the room and sit quietly. Do not participate in classroom discussions.
6. Document examples of each performance standard you observed that met, exceeded, or fell short of performance standards.

Exhibit 12.1. Instructor Assessment Tool.

Instructor: _____   Course: _____
Segment observed: _____   Date: _____
Length of observation: _____ Observer: _____

Directions:
1. Determine area of performance to be observed.
2. Observe and document instructor performance. Note if performance met (M), exceeded (E), or did not meet (NM) performance standards. Note in comments column if performance was not observed (NO) or not applicable (NA). Refer to instructor performance standards (Chapter Four) for complete descriptions of performance standards.
3. Instructors using this tool to assess themselves should complete their assessments at the end of each session and review them before the next session.

	Performance Standard	Results	Comments
1.	Preparation activities completed on time	M E NM	
2.	Course content reviewed	M E NM	
3.	Training plan prepared	M E NM	
4.	Training aids set up	M E NM	
5.	Facilities set up	M E NM	
6.	Materials available	M E NM	
7.	Supplies set in place	M E NM	
8.	Pre-course material distributed	M E NM	
9.	Trainee roster reviewed	M E NM	
10.	Relevant data reviewed	M E NM	
11.	Participation encouraged	M E NM	
12.	Instructor is accessible	M E NM	
13.	Participants' names used	M E NM	
14.	Positive reinforcement techniques used	M E NM	
15.	Minimal and overt cues reacted to appropriately	M E NM	
16.	Participants put at ease	M E NM	
17.	Control of classroom maintained	M E NM	
18.	Participants used as resources	M E NM	
19.	Instructor is unbiased	M E NM	
20.	Classroom problems handled appropriately	M E NM	
21.	Negative situations turned into positive ones	M E NM	
22.	Nervousness managed	M E NM	
23.	Eye contact is equal	M E NM	
24.	Gestures nondistracting	M E NM	
25.	Voice is clear and audible	M E NM	
26.	Training material used as a guide	M E NM	

Exhibit 12.1. Instructor Assessment Tool, Cont'd.

27.	Positive attitude demonstrated	M E NM
28.	Words are understood	M E NM
29.	Logistical items reviewed	M E NM
30.	Overviews provided	M E NM
31.	Objectives provided	M E NM
32.	Summaries and transitions provided	M E NM
33.	Instructions clearly and concisely given	M E NM
34.	Schedule followed	M E NM
35.	Material presented accurately	M E NM
36.	Material presented thoroughly	M E NM
37.	Material presented sequentially	M E NM
38.	Outline deviated from as necessary	M E NM
39.	Opportunities for review and questions provided	M E NM
40.	Open questions used appropriately	M E NM
41.	Closed questions used appropriately	M E NM
42.	Questions used to test for knowledge and skills	M E NM
43.	Answers correctly and concisely given	M E NM
44.	Unanswered questions researched and reported	M E NM
45.	Questions answered nondefensively	M E NM
46.	Questions referred to participants	M E NM
47.	Participants guided to reach answers themselves	M E NM
48.	Irrelevant questions handled appropriately	M E NM
49.	Training aids used to add to learning	M E NM
50.	Training aids used proficiently	M E NM
51.	Minor maintenance performed on training aids	M E NM
52.	Alternative aids used	M E NM
53.	Safe practices followed in using training aids	M E NM
54.	Care instructions followed in using aids	M E NM
55.	Participant performance evaluated	M E NM
56.	Feedback given	M E NM
57.	Course feedback reviewed	M E NM
58.	Items requiring action other than by instructor referred appropriately	M E NM
59.	Instructor feedback items reviewed and acted on	M E NM
60.	Performance assessed	M E NM

7. After the observation is over, review your notes and pre-
    pare to provide feedback.
8. Meet with the instructor, announce the purpose of the
    feedback session, and review the motivational feed-
    back, reinforcing performance that met and exceeded
    standards.
9. Set a time and place to review developmental feedback or,
    if appropriate, take a short break and review developmen-
    tal feedback.
10. Thank the instructor and check for clarity of under-
    standing.
11. Put observations in employee file for use in preparing
    progress reviews and the annual performance appraisal.

It may take a few sessions to become comfortable with the
instructor assessment tool, but once you do, you will have an
excellent method of carrying out your responsibility to provide
feedback to your instructors—or to assess yourself, as the case
may be.

The Progress Review

The purpose of conducting progress reviews is to reinforce
desired performance and improve performance that can be
strengthened. The instructor assessment tool (Exhibit 12.1) provides training managers with the data needed to successfully
carry out a progress review. The instructor progress review form
shown in Exhibit 12.2 provides training managers with a simple
tool to complete the review. It enables managers to provide
excellent feedback in a somewhat more formal setting than the
feedback sessions following instructor observations.
    To conduct a solid review, follow these ground rules:

1. Conduct progress reviews quarterly or more often, as
    required.
2. Use the data you collected during observations to prepare
    for the reviews.

3. Follow the guidelines for motivational and developmental feedback when conducting the reviews.
4. Document the reviews by completing the instructor progress review form.

A quarterly review is sufficient for the vast majority of instructors. New instructors or instructors experiencing performance problems may require more frequent reviews. Some training managers conduct fewer reviews with experienced instructors who generally meet performance expectations. To conduct reviews less often than quarterly is usually unsatisfactory, given that we know that desired performance is reinforced by frequent feedback. Besides, the word *quarterly* is really a misnomer in that you are actually conducting three progress reviews and one annual performance appraisal.

Preparing for a progress review is easy because you already have the data you need to conduct the review—it's contained in the instructor assessment tools you completed during your observations. To prepare for the review, simply summarize the instructor performance standards met, exceeded, and not met in part one of the instructor progress review form (Exhibit 12.2). Use part two to note progress in other areas of instructor responsibility and part three to note follow-up action required.

Follow the same steps in conducting the progress review that you followed in providing motivational and developmental feedback. In other words, use the information you collected in previous observations to provide a summary of performance standards met and exceeded (motivational feedback), take a short break, and then review those areas of performance that can be improved (developmental feedback).

Documenting the progress review is easy. Much of the documentation is completed when you prepare for the review, the rest is completed during or immediately after the review and simply includes noting instructor comments and any agreements that were made between you and the instructor. To document the progress review, follow the instructions for Exhibit 12.2. It is also an excellent tool to help you prepare the annual performance appraisal. One thing it cannot do, however,

Exhibit 12.2. Instructor Progress Review Form.

Introduction

There are three parts to the progress review form. Part one summarizes progress against performance standards observed. Part two summarizes progress made in other areas of responsibility. Part three identifies follow-up actions to be taken.

Instructions

In part one, identify performance standards that were observed during the past quarter. Write the number of times you observed each standard and note your findings. The last column is for additional comments, including external conditions that may have affected performance.

In part two, record other areas of instructor responsibility, such as administrative and special projects. In the next two columns specify the targets set in each area of responsibility and the progress made in each of these areas.

In part three, identify actions to develop or strengthen performance in parts one and two. Also note who is responsible for taking the action and the target dates.

Part One

Performance Standard	Number of Times Observed	Number of Times Met	Number of Times Exceeded	Number of Times Not Met	Comments

Part Two

Other Responsibilities	Targets Set	Progress to Date	Comments

Part Three

Follow-Up Action	Person Responsible	Target Date	Comments

is address difficult performance problems. To do this success-fully, most managers require additional help.

Difficult Performance Problems

Motivational and developmental feedback generally help in-structors avoid serious performance problems. However, there may be times when instructors do not perform according to standard despite excellent feedback following observations and at progress reviews. When this happens, you have a performance problem.

There are two tools you can use to solve performance problems. The first is the job aid contained in Figure 12.1. It consists of a series of questions designed to identify and correct the cause of the performance problem.

The second is the theme-and-cue technique, a skill-building method that I learned from Donald Tosti. It is one of the most useful management tools I know, not just because of its value in handling difficult discussions, but because it can be used productively in any type of discussion.

The theme-and-cue technique relies on three basic con-cepts: theme statements, cue lines, and recueing. A theme state-ment is simply a statement of the purpose of the discussion. An example: "You have a problem completing your preparation activities in time. This is the third occasion where your training aids have not been set up." Another example: "You have not turned in your last six end-of-course evaluations. That is far too many times to be remiss."

A cue line is the question you use to invite another person into the discussion. A good cue line for the first example above might be "What do you intend to do to complete your prepara-tion activities on time?" A good cue line for the second example might be "What will you do to get your course evaluations turned in as expected?"

Recueing is simply repeating the cue line. Recueing is often a lifesaver because one of the hardest things for a manager to do during a difficult performance discussion is to stay

Figure 12.1. How to Solve Performance Problems.

Instructions

Complete the series of questions in the left-hand column. When the questions lead you to the right-hand column, you have identified the likely solution to the problem.

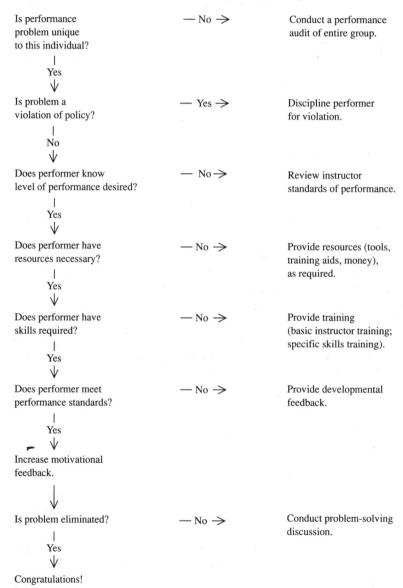

Is performance problem unique to this individual? — No → Conduct a performance audit of entire group.

Yes ↓

Is problem a violation of policy? — Yes → Discipline performer for violation.

No ↓

Does performer know level of performance desired? — No → Review instructor standards of performance.

Yes ↓

Does performer have resources necessary? — No → Provide resources (tools, training aids, money), as required.

Yes ↓

Does performer have skills required? — No → Provide training (basic instructor training; specific skills training).

Yes ↓

Does performer meet performance standards? — No → Provide developmental feedback.

Yes ↓

Increase motivational feedback.

↓

Is problem eliminated? — No → Conduct problem-solving discussion.

Yes ↓

Congratulations!

focused, and recueing helps the manager do exactly that. The following dialogue shows how valuable this tool can be.

Manager: Paul, you have been late starting class at least three or four times in the last month alone, and now your being late is a serious problem [theme statement]. I want you to tell me what you are going to do to be on time from now on [cue line].

Paul: I've been having car trouble all month long. I took my car in for service, and I still have a problem starting it on cold mornings. I don't know what to do.

Manager: I appreciate what car problems can be like; what I want to know is, what are you going to do to be on time [recue].

Paul: Well, I considered taking the bus, but you know how unreliable public transportation can be.

Manager: I understand that public transportation can be unreliable at times; however, what I want to know is, what are you going to do to be on time [recue].

Paul: Well, one day I was late because I overslept. My alarm clock didn't go off, but I got that fixed that same day.

Manager: Paul, I appreciate that you got your alarm clock fixed; but what I want to know is, what are you going to do to be on time [recue].

Paul: Well, I am on time, most of the time.

Manager: Yes, most of the time you are on time, but the times you come in late far exceed what's expected of you, so I want to know what you can do to be on time [recue].

Paul: Well, perhaps I could look into getting another car, or maybe I can carpool with some people who are more reliable than I am about being on time. At least I could carpool until I got a new car or mine fixed.

Manager: Do you think carpooling until you can purchase a new car or get yours properly fixed will get you here on time?

Paul: Yes, I do.

Manager: Great, how long will it take you to arrange a carpool?

Paul: I'll be carpooling first thing Monday morning.

Manager: That's good. I will be happy to see you here on time every day. Let's meet next Friday at this time to review how you've solved the problem.

Paul: OK, I will meet with you next Friday.

Manager: Thanks Paul, I knew you could figure this one out.

There were four examples of recueing in the above scenario. That may be more or less than you need to reach a resolution with your subordinates. At some point in these discussions, the number of recues becomes almost hilarious. There is no limit to the creative excuses people can make.

Many managers make the mistake in problem-solving discussions of asking the wrong question. More often than not, that question begins with the word *why*. "Why are you late?" is the wrong question because the employee will tell you, and then you end up discussing car trouble, public transportation, alarm clocks, babysitting, traffic, and a host of other problems that have little to do with solving the problem at hand. Recueing helps supervisors stay focused during problem-solving discussions no matter how far adrift the employee tries to take them. Occasionally, employees never do offer solutions. When that happens, give them your ideas for solving the problem. If they commit themselves to taking action on your suggestions, great; if not, then you must identify consequences for continuing the undesired behavior. If the undesired behavior goes away, you can then give the employee motivational feedback; if not, carry out the consequences.

Most problems can be successfully addressed by conducting a good problem-solving discussion. Using theme-and-cue and other good discussion techniques (listening, paraphrasing, summarizing, documenting, and so on) should help you to conduct productive discussions on the most difficult issues. If you can eliminate or reduce performance problems prior to completing the annual performance appraisal, you will be well rewarded. You will experience the pleasure of giving someone motivational feedback in an area that was previously a serious performance problem, and your overall task of preparing the annual performance appraisal and conducting the subsequent appraisal discussion will be much more pleasant.

The Annual Performance Appraisal

Many organizations have annual performance appraisal forms that they expect managers to use. Consequently, the following material has been developed to be consistent with whatever forms you may be required to use. You can integrate the concepts discussed here into any performance appraisal by either using your data as input for your appraisal or by attaching the instructor performance appraisal form (Exhibit 12.3) to your appraisal. If you don't already have an appraisal plan, you can use the one in Exhibit 12.3.

There are six steps to follow in preparing the annual performance appraisal for an instructor. You completed the first three steps when you prepared your progress review form, which is the basis of the performance appraisal.

1. Use the progress review forms (Exhibit 12.2) to document the results for each area of responsibility.
2. Review the instructor's performance with him or her to ensure completeness (recommended).
3. Note any external forces or environmental conditions that may have affected performance.
4. Determine if overall performance met, exceeded, or fell short of instructor performance standards.
5. Document the appraisal using the appropriate performance appraisal form (see Exhibit 12.3).
6. Review the appraisal with your supervisor.

Exhibit 12.3. Instructor Performance Appraisal Form.

Introduction

The performance appraisal form is a tool to document instructor performance over a given time period, generally a year. It is the formal means of providing feedback to instructors on the progress they have made in meeting performance standards.

Instructions

Part One

Attach a copy of the instructor performance standards to this appraisal form. Using the instructor progress review forms, summarize instructor performance for each area of responsibility and enter this information on the appraisal form. Make a judgment about whether the performance met, exceeded, or did not meet performance standards and circle the appropriate response. Note any unusual circumstances that may have affected instructor performance. If the instructor had responsibilities outside of the classroom, document performance results in these areas on a separate piece of paper, following a similar format.

Part Two

1. Decide whether *overall* instructor performance met, exceeded, or fell short of performance standards and check the appropriate box. Write in any comments you may want to make regarding the instructor's overall performance rating. For example, if the instructor's performance varied somewhat from the ratings, note that overall performance far exceeded expectations, somewhat exceeded expectations, fell far short of expectations, or fell somewhat short of expectations. (If you prefer to modify the form to include five overall performance categories, simply change the form to include the four examples above plus met performance expectations.)
2. Review the performance standards met and exceeded and note what the instructor did to meet and exceed those standards (motivational feedback).
3. Review the performance standards not met and note what the instructor can do to improve performance in these areas in the coming year (developmental feedback).
4. Give the instructor the opportunity to make comments on the performance appraisal (optional).
5. Sign and date the performance appraisal and ask your supervisor and the instructor to sign as well.

Instructor Performance Appraisal

Name: _____

Supervisor: _____

Phone: _____ Date: _____

Note: The instructor performance standards are attached.

Exhibit 12.3. Instructor Performance Appraisal Form, Cont'd.

Part One: Performance Summaries

Area of Responsibility: Preparation _____

_____

_____

_____

Preparation Standards: Met   Exceeded   Not Met

Area of Responsibility: Participation _____

_____

_____

_____

Participation Standards: Met   Exceeded   Not Met

Area of Responsibility: Platform Skills _____

_____

_____

_____

Platform Standards: Met   Exceeded   Not Met

Area of Responsibility: Content and Sequencing _____

_____

_____

_____

Content Standards: Met   Exceeded   Not Met

Area of Responsibility: Questioning Techniques _____

_____

_____

_____

Questioning Standards: Met   Exceeded   Not Met

Area of Responsibility: Use of Training Aids _____

_____

_____

_____

Training Aids Standards: Met   Exceeded   Not Met

Area of Responsibility: Evaluation Standards _____

_____

_____

_____

Evaluation Standards: Met   Exceeded   Not Met

Exhibit 12.3. Instructor Performance Appraisal Form, Cont'd.

Part Two: Overall Performance

1. Place a checkmark next to overall performance rating.

   Met ☐   Exceeded ☐   Did not meet ☐
   performance   performance   performance
   standards   standards   standards
   Comments: _____
   _____
   _____

2. What contributed to this individual's meeting or exceeding performance standards? _____
   _____
   _____
   _____

3. What would strengthen this individual's performance in the coming year? _____
   _____
   _____

4. Employee comments (optional): _____
   _____
   _____
   _____

5. Prepared By: _____   Date: _____
   Reviewed By: _____   Date: _____
   Employee's Signature: _____   Date: _____

The Performance Appraisal Discussion

For many managers, the performance appraisal discussion is the only discussion of performance they hold with employees. Such discussions are seldom productive and often disastrous. That's not surprising given that one performance discussion a year simply isn't enough to reinforce desired performance, let alone develop an employee who is performing at less than satisfactory levels.

Nonetheless, it is possible for these discussions to be generally easy to conduct and productive in reinforcing and developing desired performance. There are six steps to follow in conducting a successful performance appraisal discussion.

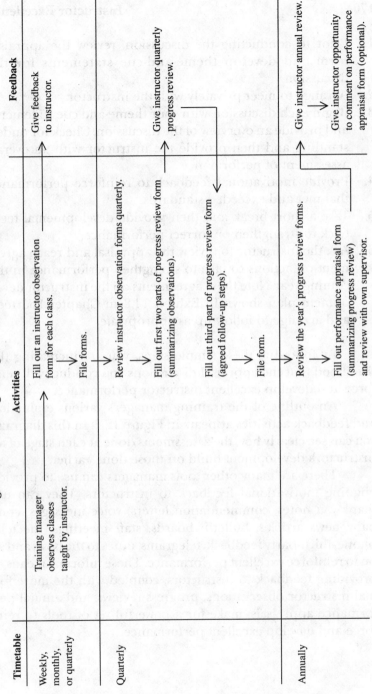

Figure 12.2. Training Manager's Guide to Providing Feedback.

Timetable	Activities	Feedback
Weekly, monthly, or quarterly	Training manager observes classes taught by instructor. → Fill out an instructor observation form for each class. → File forms.	Give feedback to instructor.
Quarterly	Review instructor observation forms quarterly. → Fill out first two parts of progress review form (summarizing observations). → Fill out third part of progress review form (agreed follow-up steps). → File form.	Give instructor quarterly progress review.
Annually	Review the year's progress review forms. → Fill out performance appraisal form (summarizing progress review) and review with own supervisor.	Give instructor annual review. Give instructor opportunity to comment on performance appraisal form (optional).

1. Prior to conducting the discussion, review the appraisal form and develop theme-and-cue statements for the discussion.
2. Arrange to meet privately with the instructor.
3. Begin each discussion with your theme-and-cue statements and provide an overview of the discussion. Check for understanding and then provide the instructor with an overall assessment of performance.
4. Provide motivational feedback to reinforce performance that met and exceeded standards.
5. Take a short break and then provide developmental feedback to strengthen or correct performance.
6. Ask the instructor to review the appraisal and reach agreement on actions to take to strengthen performance in the coming year. Note these agreements on the instructor development plan shown in Exhibit 14.2 in Chapter Fourteen and arrange to follow up as appropriate.

By following these simple steps, you are increasing the likelihood that the appraisal discussions you conduct will reinforce and develop excellent instructor performance.

An outline of the training manager's various evaluation and feedback activities appears in Figure 12.2. In this diagram, you can see clearly how the assessments done at each stage of an instructor's development build on those done earlier.

There are many other tools managers can use to provide ongoing motivational feedback to instructors. They can use thank-you notes, commendation letters, voice messages, company news articles, bulletin boards, staff meetings, the telephone, third-party feedback, telegrams, notes to the boss, and so on to reinforce excellent performance. These informal means of providing feedback to instructors, coupled with the more formal instructor observations, progress reviews, and annual performance appraisals, make for a powerful set of tools to reinforce and develop excellent performance.

13

Recognizing and Rewarding Instructors

Instructors will perform with excellence if they are recognized and rewarded for performing with excellence.

In this chapter, training managers will learn how to use recognition and rewards to reinforce desired performance and how to increase the quantity and quality of rewards without increasing budgets. If you are an instructor, this chapter will help you to position yourself to receive fair rewards and to ensure that the rewards you receive are ones that you value.

In many organizations, recognition and rewards simply do not reinforce desired performance, in part because the various programs are so poorly run. In fact, poorly run programs can have a negative impact on performance.

Making Rewards Effective

There are six key characteristics of an effective program for recognizing and rewarding instructors. They are:

1. Rewards are matched to what instructors value.
2. The right message is given.

3. The reward is appropriate to the performance.
4. Rewards and recognition are given resourcefully and creatively.
5. Rewards and recognition are given sincerely.
6. Rewards and recognition are given privately (anytime) and publicly (often).

There are many ways training managers can reward instructors. Most can be classified as either informal or formal. Informally, managers can recognize and reward people by giving praise, writing notes or letters of appreciation, giving time off, publicizing accomplishments, giving gifts, awarding certificates, and the like. The formal means of recognition and reward include compensation programs, promotion and other job movement, development, and various organizational programs that recognize outstanding individual and team performance.

Linking these forms of recognition and reward to performance increases the likelihood that the performance will be repeated and improved upon. Instructors who recognize that salary increases, bonuses, and other forms of compensation — as well as promotions, job moves, development, and the day-to-day informal rewards they receive — are directly tied to their performance will do their best to perform with excellence.

With the exception of development, most of the formal programs are so well established in most organizations that it is unlikely you can substantially change them without a rather large and time-consuming effort. Consequently, the focus of this and the next chapter is on areas that you can easily influence. This chapter focuses on the informal (day-to-day) ways of recognizing and rewarding instructors, while Chapter Fourteen focuses on the formal system of developing instructors. Let's take a close look at each of the six characteristics of an excellent recognition and reward system.

Rewards Are Matched to What Instructor Values

Training managers tend to assume that what they value is valued by instructors. This simply isn't so, and when managers act on these assumptions, they punish employees rather than reward them. Here are two examples.

Barbara enjoys her work as well as her time off. She is a fine instructor and quick to complete her classroom evaluation reports. They are consistently turned in on time, and they are accurate and well organized. Barbara's boss, Bruce, thrives on responsibility. He's impressed with Barbara's performance and says to her, "Barbara, you are so good at doing these classroom evaluation reports, I'd like you to do them for the rest of the instructor team." While Barbara ponders how she can get out of this new responsibility, Bruce walks away confident that he has just rewarded a fine instructor.

Shirley is very ambitious. She has been promoted four times in the last five years and spends what little spare time she has reading business journals. She has twelve instructors reporting to her and an opportunity to promote one of them to a demanding, yet exciting, new position in a line organization. Of the twelve, three are considered to have the potential to move up in the organization. She thinks of Sam as experienced, enthusiastic, and steady; Maria as quick, hardworking, and professional; and Bill as talented, bright, and energetic. Sam values time with his family and would consider anything that took him away from his family as a punishment. Maria absolutely loves her work, considers herself a training professional, and is determined to remain in the field. A move into a line job, even if it meant a promotion, would be considered a punishment rather than a reward. Bill, on the other hand, would jump for joy just at the prospect of being promoted. If Shirley chooses to promote Bill, she will reinforce his excellent performance. If she promotes either Sam or Maria, she will be punishing them for theirs.

There are two ways to identify what instructors value. One is to observe their reactions to informal ways you recognize and reward them and then act in accordance with their reactions. This hit-or-miss system has some value, but there is a second method that is easier and more effective. That is to simply ask them.

The Right Message Is Given

Most training managers have good intentions when it comes to recognizing and rewarding their instructors. What they don't realize is that many of the messages they send don't carry out their good intentions. Look at the example above where Bruce tells Barbara that he would like her to do all the training evaluation reports. Not only is he inadvertently punishing her for good performance, he's sending the wrong message to Barbara, as well as to other instructors who report to him. He thinks the message he's sending is "What a good job you are doing," which would have been very appropriate. The real message he's sending is "The better job you do, the more work you will be asked to do." Sending the wrong message is all too common. Let's look at another example of this.

Barry has just completed an explanation of a difficult task and has done it so well that Joyce, his training manager, is taken aback. In an effort to reinforce Barry for this excellent performance, Joyce says, "Barry, that was outstanding; I wish the rest of this instructor team could do half as well, especially Jean and Mark. They really seem to be having trouble with this lesson. I'm going to arrange for you to sit down and coach those two."

Joyce is really sending three messages here. The first message is "You did an outstanding job." The second is "I talk about others behind their backs." The third is "The better job you do, the more work you get." Joyce certainly intended to give the first message. It was straightforward and appropriate. The second message was clearly inappropriate. The third message was probably inappropriate, unless Barry did in fact perceive the assignment to be a reward or form of recognition for his outstanding performance. In all likelihood, Joyce would be surprised to learn that any part of her message did not do the job she intended.

What Joyce should have said is something like "Barry, that was outstanding. It was a very difficult lesson, yet you delivered it with such ease and clarity that the participants found it easy to do. That clearly exceeded what I expected. I think the rest of the instructor team would really find value in hearing how you handled this lesson. If you'd like, I would be more than happy to get the team together so you can present how you did this. If you don't care to do this, I'd like to pass on to them what I observed. What would you prefer?"

There are a number of messages here, all appropriate. The first message is "You did an outstanding job." The second message is "I care about the instructor staff and their development." A third message is "I will not infringe upon you simply because you have done something well." Another message is "I will let others know about your outstanding performance." Sending the right message requires training managers to consciously think about what they intend to communicate and how they will carry out their intentions.

The Reward Is Appropriate to the Performance

A trip abroad is generally not an appropriate reward for meeting performance standards, and a pat on the back is too meager an award for consistently exceeding expectations. This statement may appear obvious, but it's not. Just look at the following examples.

Company ABC introduced a new "personal best" program. The purpose of the program was to increase the quality and quantity of recognition by making it possible for employees to recognize one another for outstanding performance. The program simply required that examples of outstanding performance be documented and passed on to the supervisor of the employee being recognized. Let's look at what happened.

Ashi spent many extra weekends supplementing a training lesson that he and the other instructors were having trouble delivering successfully. After hours, he ran a program to enable the rest of the instructor staff to use the supplemental material. Not only did the revised lesson work, it actually cut out an hour of the program. Four of Ashi's peers wrote "personal best" recommendations on Ashi and sent them to Frank, Ashi's supervisor. Upon receiving the first of these, Frank took the document to Ashi and took great care to thank him. On the second occasion, he put the document on Ashi's desk without comment.

On the third occasion, he tossed the recommendation to Ashi and said rather flippantly, "What'd you do, pay them to send me these things?" The fourth document he tossed in the trash.

Joe noticed that Mary "beat" the other instructors into the office by twenty to thirty minutes each morning. Wanting to reward this behavior, he wrote an anonymous "personal best" recommendation. It had to be anonymous, he concluded, since he was Mary's supervisor. He gathered together all of the instructor and office staff and presented Mary with a cake and the "personal best" recommendation. He spoke on for some time about loyalty, dependability, dedication, and so on. Mary seemed embarrassed by his kind words, but Joe was pleased that he set such a good example.

Neither of these examples shows an appropriate response by supervisors. Had Frank taken Joe's approach and publicly recognized Ashi, he probably would have won the hearts of the entire instructor team, in addition to appropriately reinforcing Ashi's outstanding performance. It would have been appropriate for Joe to simply thank Mary for coming into work as early as she did. As it turned out, Mary arrived at work early only so that she could be the first one out of the office—a fact Joe did not know.

Rewards and Recognition Are Given Creatively and Resourcefully

When asked what form of recognition or reward they most value, most employees quickly specify money. Yet when asked to recall a time they felt especially well rewarded or recognized, the answer usually has nothing to do with money. Money, like water, tends to evaporate. Shortly after you've been given some, you want some more. While a raise or a cash bonus can serve as a short-term motivator, it seldom provides long-term satisfaction, even though a lack of money can be a tremendous source of dissatisfaction.

I've asked hundreds of employees to describe a time in their career when they felt especially well recognized or rewarded. About 5 percent of those responses had something to do with money. Most people described occasions when someone took great care to let them know their work was valued. Sometimes it was a simple thank-you, a letter to a higher-up, a spontaneous standing ovation, or a special treat or assignment. It even took the form of a letter describing the impact the employee had on the life of another person. At other times, it was a more elaborate and public form of recognition or reward, such as a formal presentation, a potluck dinner, a surprise party, a trip, or a night out on the town honoring the employee. Often these rewards came from a boss. Sometimes they came from employees or peers or participants in a class.

More often than not, these valued forms of recognition and rewards cost little or nothing. However, they require some thought and effort, and sometimes they require resourcefulness or creativity. A manager's ability to recognize and reward employees is limited only by a lack of creativity or resourcefulness, not by money. The formal mechanisms of recognition and reward (salary increases, bonuses, promotions, and so on) are usually well defined in organizations and leave little room for flexibility when it comes to giving the reward. Consequently, training managers must draw upon their own resourcefulness and creativity to find ways to recognize and reward instructors for excellent performance.

Exhibit 13.1 lists ninety-nine ways to recognize and reward instructors without adding to the manager's budget. In selecting among them, training managers must take into account what specific instructors value. Any one item may be viewed as a reward by one instructor and a punishment by another. A good way to find out what your instructors value is to show them the list and ask them to check those items that they value and add items that are not on the list.

Rewards and Recognition Are Given Sincerely

Training managers who are sincere when rewarding and recognizing instructors reinforce excellent performance. No matter how well a manager tries to cover up insincerity, it is easily spotted by the receiver. When this happens, the receiver is usually left feeling insulted.

Exhibit 13.1. Ninety-Nine Ways to Recognize and Reward Instructors.

1. ☐ simple thank-you
2. ☐ handshake
3. ☐ pat on the back
4. ☐ memo to higher-ups
5. ☐ memo to peers
6. ☐ company news article
7. ☐ private recognition
8. ☐ attendance at conference
9. ☐ time off
10. ☐ sit in for boss
11. ☐ special project
12. ☐ choice of hours
13. ☐ offer flex time
14. ☐ employee of the month
15. ☐ special parking space
16. ☐ telecommuting
17. ☐ telling a third party
18. ☐ testimonials
19. ☐ special freedom
20. ☐ more work
21. ☐ less work
22. ☐ advanced training
23. ☐ excluded from training
24. ☐ tell others about work
25. ☐ selected to lead groups
26. ☐ private phone
27. ☐ special assignment
28. ☐ choice of assignment
29. ☐ participation in decisions
30. ☐ represent company
31. ☐ represent boss at meetings
32. ☐ business trip
33. ☐ solicit instructor's ideas
34. ☐ attend company training
35. ☐ more access to information
36. ☐ redesign job
37. ☐ get to teach others
38. ☐ position as role model
39. ☐ letter to personnel file
40. ☐ note on bulletin board
41. ☐ better equipment
42. ☐ additional supplies
43. ☐ publicizing accomplishments
44. ☐ floor meeting recognition
45. ☐ something named for person
46. ☐ put on accelerated program
47. ☐ waiver from procedures
48. ☐ use of voice mail
49. ☐ gifts
50. ☐ more responsibility
51. ☐ less responsibility
52. ☐ new title
53. ☐ card
54. ☐ standing ovation
55. ☐ good job move
56. ☐ added time with boss
57. ☐ more observing time
58. ☐ less observing time
59. ☐ facilitate training
60. ☐ photo display
61. ☐ special support
62. ☐ visible projects
63. ☐ important projects
64. ☐ motivational feedback
65. ☐ certificates
66. ☐ letters of appreciation
67. ☐ given preferred duties
68. ☐ more varied duties
69. ☐ more creative tasks
70. ☐ increased authority
71. ☐ set own goals
72. ☐ schedule self
73. ☐ coupons
74. ☐ homebaked item
75. ☐ status symbols
76. ☐ inclusion in meetings
77. ☐ exclusion from meetings
78. ☐ time with higher-ups
79. ☐ picture in newspaper
80. ☐ more office space
81. ☐ party
82. ☐ potluck
83. ☐ free meal
84. ☐ gold stars
85. ☐ post results
86. ☐ commendations displayed
87. ☐ exposure to top management
88. ☐ commendations forwarded
89. ☐ work examples displayed
90. ☐ nomination for awards
91. ☐ relief from aversive work
92. ☐ approval of requests
93. ☐ self-management
94. ☐ more requests for input
95. ☐ given promotional items
96. ☐ recommendations accepted
97. ☐ flowers from the garden
98. ☐ handmade presents
99. ☐ company outings

Rewards and Recognition Are Given Privately (Anytime) and Publicly (Often)

To reward and recognize instructors privately is always appropriate; to do so publicly is appropriate so long as it does not terribly embarrass the receiver. When you publicly reward and recognize instructors you are sending several messages. First, you are saying that you value what the instructor has accomplished; second, that you care enough about excellent performance to take the time to reinforce it; and third, that excellent performance is the model for other instructors within the organization. If an instructor would be greatly embarrassed by such public reinforcement, then it is best to reward or recognize the individual privately.

Occasionally supervisors fear that any form of recognition or reward above and beyond what is absolutely required will cause employees to expect more and more. In my experience, this seldom happens. Employees who receive abundant recognition and rewards are genuinely grateful about what they receive and realistic about their expectations for more.

The five steps to recognizing and rewarding instructors are essentially the same ones you follow to provide motivational feedback.

Step 1. Provide the reward or recognition immediately following or as close to the performance as practical. Most informal forms of recognition and rewards can be given immediately following performance. Some of the more formal ones, like compensation, are given at set times; these you should arrange for as soon as you can.

Step 2. Link the reward or recognition to the performance you observed or monitored. Specifically describe the performance.

Step 3. Tie the performance to the job expectations. Let the instructor know what expectations were addressed by the performance.

Step 4. Explain how the performance met or exceeded expectations. Let the instructor know that the reward or recognition is a consequence of meeting or exceeding performance expectations.

Step 5. Encourage the individual to continue this kind of performance.

Instructor Responsibility for Rewards

Many instructors feel helpless when it comes to taking responsibility for the rewards they receive. Nonetheless, the fact is that instructors can affect the rewards they receive, as the following story demonstrates.

Each December, Bob would arrange to meet with his boss. He would tell his boss that it was his intention to be an outstanding performer and that he had developed a set of objectives for the coming year. He would say that he wanted to review them with his boss to be sure that everything his boss wanted done was included and that none of the objectives were inappropriate. He would proceed to add and delete objectives, as appropriate. He would then ask his boss to imagine that the coming year was at an end and that Bob had successfully completed the objectives set. Would his boss view Bob's performance as having met, exceeded, or fallen short of what he expected? Bob's desire was to exceed his boss's expectations so, depending upon the answer to his question, he would either ask, "What do I need to add to this list to exceed your expectations?" or, "I'm glad you said 'exceeded,' because that is exactly what I want to do." He would then say, "To make it easy for you to know that I am on track, I will document the progress I make toward these objectives and review the documentation with you each quarter. That should also make it easy for you to document my performance appraisal." Bob knew that as long as he stuck to his program (met his objectives and carried out his commitments), he would receive an outstanding performance appraisal and the rewards that accompany an outstanding performance rating.

In effect, what Bob was doing was implementing an employee-driven performance appraisal system in an organization without one. If your company does not have such a system, you can use what you've learned here to let your boss know what you intend to accomplish in the coming year and implement your own performance plan to ensure that you receive adequate rewards. If your company does have such a system, be aggressive in endorsing it and finding ways to make it easy for your boss to successfully implement it. For example, take the time to document progress you make toward your objectives. Instructors can't guarantee that they will receive adequate rewards, but they can take responsibility for putting themselves in positions that make it likely.

The same can be said for ensuring that the rewards received are valued ones. Earlier, you read that the best way for training managers to know what rewards instructors value is to ask them. However, you don't have to wait to be asked to let your training manager know what rewards you value. If a reward for you is time off, let your manager know. If your big reward is a promotion, let your manager know. If your reward is staying where you are in a field of work that you love, let your manager know. When it comes to the many informal means of recognition and reward, use Exhibit 13.1 to let your manager know which of the ninety-nine items on the list you value. This may be uncomfortable for you, but use common sense and do it anyway. Most managers will appreciate knowing what you value; those who don't appreciate it need to know anyway.

By making the best use of existing reward and recognition programs, training managers can find many ways to reinforce excellent performance by instructors. Although it is difficult to substantially affect most of an organization's formal reward program, there is one area that can be easily affected: instructor development, the focus of the next chapter.

14

Developing Instructors and Their Careers

Instructors will perform with excellence if they are developed to perform with excellence.

In this chapter, training managers will learn how to develop instructors to perform with excellence in their current and future jobs, and instructors will learn how to take responsibility for their own professional development. In most organizations, development, if it even exists, is generally aimed at the stars and the fast-trackers of the group. This is a serious mistake. Most instructors, like most employees, aren't stars or fast-trackers. What this means is that most instructors do not receive any development, regardless of how well they perform. When development does occur, it is most always self-initiated.

Development is a means to create excellent performance in all instructors. As such, it is not just a way of moving up. It is also a way of moving sideways, staying in place, or even moving backwards.

A good development system helps training managers and instructors carry out their respective responsibilities for development. We'll look at development first from the training manager's point of view and then from the instructor's point of view. Let's begin by looking at the ten characteristics of excellent development.

1. It is a responsibility of both training managers and instructors.
2. It is an ongoing process rather than a single act.
3. It is based on the instructor's performance and potential, rather than on the manager's ability to "sell."
4. It addresses all instructors, not just the stars.
5. It bases appropriate development steps on the instructor's performance, potential, and aspirations.
6. It is realistic and enhanced by the agreement of higher management.
7. It recognizes that "up" is not the only way.
8. It respects differences in instructors and their values.
9. It is conducted in private, yet openly and genuinely.
10. It is documented in a development plan.
11. It begins on day one.

In the following pages, you will explore the impact that these characteristics have upon the development and performance of instructors.

Responsibility for Development

Responsibility for instructor development is not a shared responsibility. Instructors are 100 percent responsible for their own development, and training managers are 100 percent responsible for the development of their instructors. Training managers are responsible for the development of all instructors, not just the stars and fast-trackers. Instructors should not read this to mean that their supervisors will take care of them. The idea that "the company takes care of you" is long extinct. Instructors who initiate and carry out their own development will come away with a clear sense of who they are, where they are headed, and how to get there.

Although development is an ongoing process rather than

a single act, many managers look upon development as something that occurs annually, usually to meet an organizational goal or commitment. When development is treated as an annual event, it is unlikely to have much effect on performance. This is akin to exercising once a year and believing that the event has much to do with your state of physical fitness.

If managers look at development as an ongoing event, they will recognize how development affects performance. For example, motivational feedback, developmental feedback, informal recognition, progress reviews, and annual discussions of performance and development are all a part of the developmental process. By implementing the instructor performance system in this book, training managers will be able to treat development as an ongoing process.

Unfortunately, in most organizations, development simply does not take place. When it does, it is usually thought of in terms of promoting people. This is a mistake, which is usually played out in the following way. Each manager is given an opportunity to tell why his or her employee should be promoted. Since managers often consider it a feather in their cap to get to do this, they quickly learn that the way to get employees promoted is to "sell them" and attack the weakness of other candidates for promotion. The end results are often disastrous because the promotion decision has more to do with the manager's sales ability than it does with the candidate's performance and potential. Promotions, like all other forms of development (lateral job moves, staying in the current position, temporary assignments, special project work, downgrading, and so on) should be based on performance and potential.

Rating Performance and Potential

Judging performance is easy. Simply use the instructor's performance record (appraisal and progress reviews) to rate his or her performance on the following scale.

Scale for Rating Performance

VH = Very High
H = High

MH = Medium High
M = Medium
ML = Medium Low
L = Low
VL = Very Low
U = Unknown (too little evidence to
evaluate performance)

Some organizations conduct formal assessment programs that provide data which can be used to judge an employee's potential. If you have this capability, then the data you
need to make such judgments are at your fingertips. However,
most organizations don't have access to assessment centers.
When such data are lacking, use your best judgment and the
judgment of others to determine the movement potential of
instructors: up, sideways, stationary, down, or out. Although
these judgments are not scientific, they are the judgments managers make daily. The following scale provides a practical way of
making these judgments.

Scale for Rating Potential

Very High (VH) = potential to move up two levels
High (H) = clear potential to move up one level, maybe
two
Medium High (MH) = potential to move up one level only
Medium (M) = may or may not be able to move up one
level; can grow in current level
Medium Low (ML) = unlikely to move up
Low (L) = will not move up
Very Low (VL) = will not move up; may move laterally or
downward
Unknown (U) = too little evidence to judge

Factors to consider in making these judgments include
capability, aptitude, experience, and style. How you rate the
performance and judge the potential of instructors will help you
decide how best to develop them.

Development Groups

From a development point of view, there are roughly six different groupings of instructors, ranging from those who are high performers and are judged to be going higher in the organization to those who are low performers and are judged not to be going any higher. There is also a group considered either too new or too invisible to rate in terms of either performance or potential.

By limiting development to those individuals who are considered to be going somewhere, managers do a gross disservice to the rest of the employee population, as well as to themselves. Consider for a minute those employees who are high performers but who are not going to move up in the organization. It is absolutely criminal not to develop this group of high performers. They are often the core of an organization, the experts and the professionals. Their continued excellent performance is dependent, in part, on such reinforcement.

Effective development begets effective performance; consequently, to limit the development of any single group of performers is downright dumb. If excellent performers do not have the opportunity to stay abreast of their profession, to keep up their expertise, and so forth, their performance is likely to plummet. The following identifies each of the development groups.

Identifying Developmental Groups

High Performance/ High Potential — These are the stars and fast-trackers, excellent performers who are judged to be moving up in the organization.

High Performance/ Low Potential — These are good, solid performers who are judged not to be going any higher. They are often people who have reached a high level of expertise or professionalism. They may be at the pinnacle of their career. They may stay in place or move laterally.

Low Performance/ High Potential	These are people, usually few in number, who are having trouble in their current assignment but are judged to have potential to move up. They are almost always mismatched to their jobs.
Low Performance/ Low Potential	This is a group of performers who are performing at low levels and are judged to have little or no potential to move up. They may stay in place, move laterally, drop back, or leave.
Unknown Performance and/or Potential	These are people who are either too new in the organization to be rated or who are in invisible (remote) jobs.
Medium Performance or Potential	These are people whose performance or potential hovers between high and low. I suggest that you treat them as if their performance or potential is high. If, after a year or so, they do not clearly demonstrate high performance or high potential, then put them into one of the other groupings.

No grouping is more important than another when it comes to development. What is important is that training managers reinforce and develop all groups to perform in one of the high-performance categories. To do this requires training managers to identify specific development steps for each of these groups. For example, any development activity that prepares an instructor for upward movement is appropriate only for those instructors who are considered to be high performers with high potential to move ahead. Development steps that are intended to reinforce excellent performance are perfect for the high performer who is not moving forward. Exhibit 14.1 identifies the appropriate development steps for each group of instructors. As you can see, the development steps suggested for each

Exhibit 14.1. Appropriate Development Steps.

Performance/ Potential Grouping	Appropriate Development Steps
High Performance/ High Potential	• Promotion • More responsibility • More decision-making powers • Exposure to other business areas • Opportunity to manage • Increased span of supervison • Key job assignments • High-risk job assignments • Key job moves • Lateral move to prepare for promotion • Important special project • Educational experiences that prepare for future advancement • Anything upward
High Performance/ Low Potential	• Opportunities to update skills or knowledge • Experiences that enable instructors to stay abreast of their field of expertise • Attendance at professional conferences • Involvement in professional groups • Being selected to represent organization to others inside and outside the organization • Opportunities for advanced training • Public recognition
Low Performance/ High Potential	• Skills training • Quick job move to match skills • Change in supervision • Opportunity to gain knowledge of the business
Low Performance/ Low Potential	• Another chance in same or different job under same or different supervisor • Downgrading • Outplacement
Unknown Performance and/or Potential	• Time in job • Visible work assignments or special projects • Exposure to decision makers • Periodic review of work
Medium Performance or Potential	• Treat as you would those with high performance or potential initially • Treat as you would those with low performance or potential thereafter

group of performers differ widely. By applying appropriate development steps, you increase the likelihood that all instructors will remain in or move into one of the high-performance categories.

Reaching Agreement on Development

To be effective, development must be realistic, and to be realistic, it must be based upon agreement at higher levels. If development plans are put together by instructors and their training managers without the agreement of higher management, the likelihood of these plans being realized is not very great. Nothing is more damaging to future performance than for employees to spend a year or more carrying out a development plan put together with their training manager only to have the training manager's boss say, "I don't agree."

It is even more effective if the agreement extends to the training manager's peers. There are two reasons for this. First, these peers generally hold views about the performance and potential of all the instructors. Regardless of their validity, these views will affect the development of the instructors. By formalizing peer involvement in the development process, the training manager has the opportunity to correct invalid perceptions as well as to bring valid concerns out into the open. Second, by involving peers, the training manager is getting several people to focus their attention on the development of each instructor. This will increase the likelihood that developmental activities will come about as planned.

Frankly, most training managers have never experienced a productive development session (one based upon agreement). Most development sessions that managers participate in are based upon disagreement. As we saw earlier, those sessions are typically conducted to determine who will be promoted. They typically begin with training managers presenting their own candidates (and knocking down any others) and end with the boss picking the candidate whose training manager does the best selling job. There are five steps you can take to gain agreement on a development plan.

Step 1. The training manager and the boss and peers of the training manager should be given a list of instructors and asked to rate the performance and potential of each instructor anonymously, using the rating scales given previously. This can be done in advance of a scheduled meeting or at the beginning of the meeting.

Step 2. Without comment, the boss posts the ratings for all to see. Executing this step as it is stated is critical. Posting ratings without comment reduces the managers' need to be defensive and increases the likelihood that disagreements will be resolved easily.

Step 3. The boss circles those names where there is basic agreement. For example, if you rate an instructor as a very high performer and your peers rate that instructor as a high performer, you are in basic agreement. If you rate an instructor as a high performer and a peer rates the same instructor as a medium or medium-low performer, you are not in basic agreement because you are more than one step apart. More than likely, there will be agreement on most (if not all) of the names on the list.

Step 4. Everyone should discuss those names where there is no agreement and come to a consensus rating decision. Begin by checking out whether the opinions expressed are strongly held. This will help the group come to agreement, as often some of the more divergent views expressed are not strongly held. This process enables people to change their views without feeling they are cemented to them. If agreement can't be reached, defer to those who know the instructor best. This usually includes the instructor's supervisor.

Step 5. Once agreement is reached on the ratings for all instructors, use Exhibit 14.1 to identify the appropriate development steps for each instructor and identify what each participant can do to support the plans developed.

This process weeds out the vast majority of problems usually associated with developmental sessions. Because this process is based upon agreement rather than competitive positioning or sales skills, these sessions seldom turn into disaster. Over and over again, managers have been astounded at how productive these sessions can be. By having a team of managers in agreement on the development of each instructor, you increase the likelihood that development plans will come to life.

Forms of Development

In most organizations, when people talk about development, they talk in terms of upward movement. However, the fact is that upward movement is only one form of development. Staying in place, moving sideways, and even moving downward are all legitimate forms of development.

By thinking of development only in terms of upward movement, managers inadvertently send the message that all other forms of development are suspect. Frankly, it's hard to imagine an organization that would truly want all of its employees clamoring to get to the top. The resulting frustration would be enough to topple most organizations. When managers validate other forms of development, the stigmas associated with them disappear.

For instructors who do aspire to move higher in the organization and who are judged to have the capability to do so, there is no problem. Managers simply have to treat these individuals as they would any high-performance, high-potential employee. This may include promotions, but it may also include good lateral job moves in preparation for a future promotion. Occasionally, it may include stepping back to take an assignment that provides the employee with expertise needed to move forward.

Managers need to respect the aspirations of instructors who want to remain in the training field. Managers should develop these instructors as they would other high performers who are not moving forward in the organization.

Managers should treat instructors who are having trouble in their assignments as they would others who are performing below standard. That is, they should arrange a quick, lateral job move for instructors mismatched to their jobs and pursue downgraded assignments for those instructors who are poor performers and who are judged not to be moving forward in the organization. For some, these moves may not look like development because they are so uncomfortable. However, development is sometimes uncomfortable, and in these cases training managers need to manage the discomfort to the best of their abilities.

Many workers in the early to mid twentieth century could be neatly categorized as "company loyalists." These individuals tended to do what they were told without question and believed the company would take care of them. They were thrilled to know they had a job for the rest of their working life. They valued security above all else—and with good reason. Having a secure job meant that they could find shelter, feed and educate their children, and probably live and die with some dignity and respect. Staying in place was all the development this group of people required.

Workers today are as diverse as their values. They are people of all ages, colors, religions, and cultures. They are men and women, straight and gay, abled and disabled. They are married and single; they include single parents and dual-income couples. They speak different languages, attain different educational levels, and represent divergent beliefs.

There are still company loyalists. In addition, there are others who work because they love the work itself and those who work because work provides them with the money that enables them to do what they really want to do in life, whether it be sailing, acting, gardening, or simply spending time with their families. Some of these people want to move up the corporate ladder; others clearly do not. By recognizing and respecting these diversities, managers can develop their employees in ways those employees value.

The Importance of Privacy

Developmental discussions are very personal and must be conducted privately to avoid any form of embarrassment and to avoid unnecessary and potentially damaging competitiveness. To conduct these sessions publicly is to ask for poor performance.

In Chapter Twelve, you read that for feedback to be effective, it must be given sincerely. This principle holds true for development discussions: what is communicated must be genuine. This means that if an instructor aspires to be a training manager or a vice president and the team of managers who make development decisions do not see the employee as having potential to make such a move, the employee should be told so. For many managers this will be new behavior. Frankly, however, it makes more sense than dangling a carrot in front of someone you know isn't going to go anywhere. It is important that managers develop their skill in conducting these kinds of discussions (a topic that is explored later in this chapter).

The Development Plan

A documented development plan serves to formalize the development process. It is a tool that can be used to plan, monitor, and assess developmental progress. It is prepared by the training manager with input from the instructor and the training manager's peers and boss.

    The instructor development plan in Exhibit 14.2 is an easy tool to use in planning and carrying out development activities and discussions. It is also a useful tool for reviewing instructor development with your boss and peers and one you can begin using the first day the instructor appears on the job. Beginning development of instructors on their first day goes a long way toward developing and retaining excellent performance. In most organizations, development, if it exists at all, begins when a problem arises. Yet during interviews, most training managers note instructor skills that require strengthening. The time to begin exploring development of these areas is immediately. Let's look at two scenarios.

    Jane has just selected Brent as her new instructor. She tells Brent she's happy to have him on board and proceeds to tell him all about the job and the organization he has joined. Jane selected Brent because he was the best candidate available. Although she was somewhat suspicious of his decision-making skills, she decided not to say anything about them since he is so new and she wasn't able to clearly pinpoint her concern. "If he

Exhibit 14.2. Instructor Development Plan.

Instructions

Begin by filling out the data required at the top of the form. Then complete Section 1 (long-term career interests) by gathering input from the instructor. To complete Section 2, refer to the list of instructor requirements from Exhibit 2.1, the various feedback tools (Exhibits 12.1, 12.2, and 12.3 and Figure 12.1), and data collected from the developmental session conducted with your peers and boss. You can use this same information plus suggestions from the instructor to complete Section 3. To complete Section 4, note what, if any, job movement is planned in the near future. Finally, note the dates of development reviews and follow-up discussions.

Name: _____   Organization: _____

Title: _____   Time in Job: _____

Performance/Potential Rating: _____

---

1.   Long-Term Career Interests:

---

2.   Skills or Knowledge Requiring Development:

---

3.   Specific Actions: Timetable:

---

4.   Short-Term Focus (Remain in current job, lateral move, promotion, other):

First discussion held on: _____/_____/_____
Follow-up discussions held on: _____/_____/_____

has a problem, I'll find out about it," she thought. She was right. Not six months passed before Jane began to hear a number of complaints from trainees about classes starting late and being canceled without notice. Upon further investigation, Jane found out that Brent started every class late, waiting anywhere from five to thirty minutes before beginning. In addition, she discovered that Brent had canceled three programs within the last month alone and on one of these occasions had failed to give any notice whatsoever. All of a sudden, Jane has a serious performance problem on her hands.

It is typical of training managers not to say anything when they suspect a particular skill problem. Instead, they wait and see if what they suspect actually becomes a problem. Nine out of ten times it does. At that point, the training manager faces the often difficult task of trying to correct the performance problem.

Now look at the same scenario, but with a twist. Jane selects Brent as a new instructor. She is very pleased with this selection, as Brent possesses a number of excellent skills and was clearly the best candidate she interviewed. She is concerned about his decision-making abilities, although she can't exactly pinpoint her concern. She has invited Brent to meet with her on his first day on the job.

Jane tells Brent that she is thrilled he has accepted the assignment and adds that he was clearly the best candidate she interviewed. She then proceeds to let him know that she wants to review all the skills she was able to see as a result of the interview and follow up by exploring areas that either or both of them would like to see him develop. She goes through the long list of skills and qualifications that contributed to his being selected and asks Brent if he has any questions. He says no.

Jane then says that she wants them to explore areas of skill that, if strengthened, would increase the likelihood of his being a successful instructor. She asks if he has any questions, and he says no. Jane then tells Brent that coming away from the inter-view she sensed that he might need to develop his skill in decision making. She asks him if decision making is an area he would like to develop. He proceeds to tell her that decision making is a skill he has wanted to work on for some time now but that he hasn't felt comfortable telling anyone lest they think he was lousy at making decisions. She thanks him for his candor, and they reach agreement on a training program specifically aimed at developing such skills. Brent develops into a fine instructor who starts classes on time and doesn't cancel them inappropriately.

The primary difference in the above two scenarios is that in one Jane addressed the problem before it arose and in the other she waited until after it had arisen. By beginning development on day one, she was able to help Brent develop his decision-making skills before experiencing performance problems. By addressing development on day one, she also made it clear to Brent that he could talk to her about potential problems without fear of reprisal.

Steps to Effective Development

There are six steps training managers can take to ensure successful development of instructors.

Step 1. Evaluate the instructor's performance and judge his or her potential, using the rating systems described in this chapter.

Step 2. Prepare a preliminary development plan, using the list of developmental groups, the list of appropriate development steps, and Exhibit 14.2. It's a good idea also to refer to Exhibits 2.1, 12.2, and 12.3 and Figure 12.1.

Step 3. Gain appropriate agreement with your boss and peers on instructor performance ratings and judgments of potential. Follow the steps to reach agreement on instructor development outlined in this chapter and complete the instructor development plan in Exhibit 14.2.

Step 4. Prepare for the career discussion. Review the results of steps one through three, determine the kind of discussion you are going to have, and develop your theme-and-cue statements.

Step 5. Conduct the career discussion. Confirm the instructor's aspirations and resolve any differences. Revise (if appropriate) and reach agreement on the instructor development plan.

Step 6. Monitor progress. Conduct follow-up sessions as appropriate and monitor progress toward the objectives outlined in the instructor development plan.

Steps one through three have been already covered in this chapter. Consequently, the focus here will be on steps four, five, and six. Let's begin with step four.

Preparing for the Career Discussion

To prepare for the career discussion, the training manager needs to review the material from steps one, two, and three, above. Then the training manager needs to determine the type of discussion to hold. There are four possibilities: announcement, fact finding, agreement, and problem solving.

Announcement is a perfect form of communication when you have the task of telling someone something over which they have no real choice. Outplacement or downgrading are examples of when this form of communication is required. In these instances, the training manager simply makes the necessary announcement and checks to see that the instructor understands it.

Fact finding is the right form of discussion to use when training managers want to identify the instructor's aspirations or development plans. In fact-finding discussions, training managers state the purpose of the discussion and proceed to ask instructors to provide the facts.

Agreement is the ideal form of discussion when training managers want instructors to work with them to do something. Making joint decisions on appropriate development steps is a good example of an agreement discussion. In an agreement discussion, the training manager announces the purpose of the discussion and then asks participants to offer their ideas, suggestions, and so forth, in an effort to reach agreement.

Problem solving is the right form of discussion to use when you have a performance problem or a development problem. For example, this kind of discussion would be held with instructors who consistently fail to keep agreements. In problem-solving discussions, training managers state the problem and then proceed to ask instructors what they are going to do to solve it.

Once training managers identify the kind of discussion they are going to conduct, they need to develop their theme-and-cue statements. As you may recall from Chapter Twelve, a theme statement is a statement of the purpose of the discussion. A cue line is the question you use to invite the other person into the discussion. Recueing is simply repeating the cue line. Let's look at how these statements can be used effectively in the four types of discussion.

Announcement. An example of a good theme statement for this type of discussion would be something like "The purpose of this meeting is to let you know that you are scheduled to attend a four-hour career exploration session in the company cafeteria this coming Monday." A good cue line for this theme statement might be "Do you need any other information to get to the session?" Another example of a theme statement for an announcement discussion might be "On the first of April, the company will be introducing a series of employee development workbooks, which are intended to help you focus your current and future development." This can be followed up using a cue line something like "Can you tell me what's being introduced?"

Fact Finding. One example of a theme statement for a fact-finding discussion is "The purpose of this session is to begin discussing your career development." This may be followed up with the cue line "Can you tell me what you aspire to do in your career?" Another example: "I've had a couple of people tell me they simply didn't understand the point of the first morning lecture [theme statement]. Can you tell me if this is typical or simply a fluke [cue line]?"

Agreement. "The purpose of this meeting is to set objectives for introducing the new employee development workbooks" is a good theme statement for an agreement discussion. "What targets do you have in mind?" is a good follow-up cue line. Another example: "Lucy, I would like to use this time for the two of us to come up with a list of ways to make you more competitive for that sales job you desire [theme statement]. What thoughts do you have about this [cue line]?"

Problem Solving. A good example of a theme statement and cue line for this type of discussion is "Perry, you have been late four times this past month, and on each occasion we have lost trainees as a result. As you know, that exceeds what is acceptable and is posing a problem in the classroom [theme statement]. I want to know what you are going to do to be on time every day [cue line]." Another good example: "Shirley, you are using closed questions to try and open up discussions, which simply isn't working, as you are getting very little response from participants. We have discussed how to use closed questions on two other occasions, yet I do not see a change in your questioning techniques. This is a problem because it does not meet what is expected of you [theme statement]. I want to know what you are going to do to correct the problem [cue line]." A third example: "Ali, you want to move into the senior instructor position, yet you haven't arranged to attend the company training required to be a senior instructor, nor have you gone outside the company to develop equivalent skills. You have got to do one or the other to be a senior instructor [theme statement]. What I want to know is, what are you going to do about it [cue line]?"

By developing a good theme statement for developmental discussions, you will ensure that your discussions are clear and to the purpose. By developing a good cue line, you will direct the way instructors participate, and by recueing and preparing for potential problems, you will keep the discussion focused. Once you have determined the type of development discussion to hold and have written your theme-and-cue statements, you are ready to conduct the career discussion.

Conducting the Career Discussion

If this is your first career development discussion with employees, begin by conducting a fact-finding discussion to identify their aspirations. If this is a subsequent discussion, begin by confirming their aspirations. The second part of the discussion is likely to be an announcement. This is where you let employees know whether their aspirations and the management team's perceptions of their abilities are in agreement. For example, if the instructor aspires to move up two levels in the organization and the management team perceives the instructor as having that potential, then everyone's perceptions are in agreement and the instructor should be told so. However, if the management team does not think the employee has the ability to move beyond the current level, then everyone's perceptions are not in agreement and the employee should be told this as well.

The next step in the discussion may be agreement or problem solving, depending upon whether a problem emerged in the preceding part of the discussion. If there was no problem or if any problems were satisfactorily resolved, then the discussion should proceed to the agreement phase, in which you jointly identify development steps that are appropriate for the instructor's aspirations or the management team's perceptions. This step should enable you to complete a final draft of the instructor development form in Exhibit 14.2. If problems were not resolved, then give the instructor some time to think about the feedback before proceeding. Eventually, either agreements are reached regarding development or the training manager simply announces the development steps the instructor must follow.

Finally, training managers should schedule progress reviews to ensure that the development activities are being carried out as scheduled and to make alterations to plans, as necessary.

Monitoring Progress

A plan is only as good as the people who make it work. Consequently, training managers must monitor progress toward the attainment of the instructor development plan on a regular basis. A quarterly review is sufficient for most instructors. Training managers may want to monitor developmental progress of new instructors more frequently.

Monitoring progress toward developmental goals is an important step in the development program. By monitoring progress, training managers increase the likelihood that development plans will come to fruition and that instructors will develop into excellent performers.

In all three of the last steps of instructor development (preparing for the career discussion, conducting the discussion, and monitoring progress) instructors too have a responsibility. That responsibility includes preparing for development discussions, carrying out the development activities agreed on, and monitoring progress toward achievement of the instructor development plan. By taking responsibility for these steps, instructors can do much to ensure that these plans come to life.

Training Instructors

One of the most common forms of instructor development is training. Training is required to equip new instructors with the skills and knowledge to deliver training in accordance with the instructor performance standards and to help experienced instructors develop and strengthen their repertoire of skills. Let's take a look at this form of development before we explore the instructor's responsibility for development.

Instructors can expect to participate in an array of training programs. These include basic and advanced train-the-trainer programs, courses in specific subjects, specified skill development programs, seminars, company programs, and courses intended to prepare them for other assignments.

While all of the above programs have their part in developing excellent instructors, none is as important as the program to equip instructors to deliver training in accordance with specified standards of performance—the basic train-the-trainer program. An up-front investment in a good train-the-trainer program will yield long-term benefits in the form of excellent long-term performance.

There are hundreds of programs that are touted as good train-the-trainer programs but only a handful that actually do the job. Many programs simply focus on presentation skills. Others tend to put forth outmoded training methods. Some do a partial job; few are complete.

Training managers can assess the quality of these programs by how well they equip instructors to deliver training in accordance with the instructor performance standards listed in Chapter Four. A good train-the-trainer program will equip instructors to effectively prepare for class, gain participation, employ questioning techniques, develop platform skills, meet content and sequencing standards, use training aids, and evaluate instruction. To know how well a particular program does the job, training managers must thoroughly review course objectives and mesh these with the performance standards in Chapter Four. Reviewing course objectives is key to selecting all good training programs, whether they be designed to provide basic or advanced instructor training, to build skills, or to prepare instructors for future assignments.

Instructor Responsibility for Development

You are responsible for your own development. It may help you to know what you can expect to go through as you proceed through this lifelong and sometimes difficult process.

You can expect to go through several different stages of development in your career. First, you will go through a period of *assessment*, when you take a look at who you are and what you aspire to become. Then, you will go through a period of *exploration*, when you begin to explore potential areas of work and even try out a few before you move to the next stage, which is *growth*. Growth is the stage where your development seems rapid. It is a period of great accomplishment, usually accompanied by hard work and great excitement. It is followed by a time of *settling down* or leveling off, when accomplishments seem to come easily. You feel comfortable in your work and are at the pinnacle of your career. In the latter part of this stage, it is likely that you will feel bored or restless and begin to ask yourself questions like "Is this something I want to do for the rest of my life?" This stage is often followed by a period of *decline*. Decline is a time when accomplishments come with difficulty and you're likely to feel caught up in a downward spiral. It is a period of development often characterized by feelings of great discomfort and a fervent desire to get out of what you are doing. It is likely to lead in to a new assessment stage, thus beginning the cycle over again.

You can expect to go through these stages of development over and over again, during your career. By acknowledging that these developmental stages exist and by identifying your current stage of development, you can begin to make some good development and career decisions. By making good developmental decisions, you may be able to shorten the periods of decline in your life.

Choosing the kind of work to devote your life to and pursuing developmental experiences that support your choices are among the most important decisions you will be called upon to make as your career unfolds. There are some tools available that can help you make solid development decisions. The right ones will depend upon your current stage of development. Let's look at some examples.

Instructors who are in the assessment stage will find self-assessment tools valuable. These are usually workbooks that guide you through a serious look at who you are and what you want to be. A good self-assessment workbook will enable you to assess your fields of interest, aspirations, skills, strengths, weaknesses, characteristics, values, performance, and supervisory feedback. It will also help you to pinpoint discrepancies and reconcile differences. A self-assessment workbook is right for you if you could use some help thinking through these assessments and considering their career implications. These workbooks can be found in bookstores, libraries, and career resource centers.

Instructors who are in the exploration stage will find value in workbooks and publications that help them get information about the types of work done in the world at large and in their organization in particular. These publications, which are also available at bookstores, libraries, and career resource centers, will provide you with knowledge of alternatives essential for sound planning for your future. They should help you identify the kinds of organizations that require your skills, work experiences, and educational background. They should help you pick out organizations that exhibit values important to you and help you identify organizational norms and potential job fits. They should equip you to make good use of your network and show you how you can use your supervisor, counselors, and other employees to gain information to help you make decisions about moving up, moving across, staying in place, or moving out.

Once you have completed your assessment and exploration, you're ready to draw upon the data gathered and develop a plan for yourself. There are many publications available in the above-mentioned places to guide you through this effort. A good career planning tool should help you match your values, skills, and characteristics with organizational requirements. A good workbook will guide you to make clear decisions about whether to stay in or leave your current job and enable you to develop a realistic plan to make your decision work.

When you have completed this work, you will be well prepared for a serious and realistic career discussion with your training manager. Instructors who see themselves in one of the other three stages (growth, settling down, or decline) may also find value in the development work described above.

If you are in the growth stage, you probably want to focus your efforts on developing in your current work. If you are in the early stages of settling down, now is the perfect time to take a serious look at your development because you're typically on top of the world when it comes to work and because the hard task of development can keep you fresh in your current work and out of the slide into decline. If you are in the latter stages of settling down or in decline, you have no choice but to begin a serious look into your development and career or fall deeper into discontent.

The developmental work described here isn't easy, nor can it be done quickly without doing injustice to your career. However, if you take the time to do this work, and do it seriously, you will be rewarded with a career full of satisfaction.

Instructors who take responsibility for their own development will develop into excellent performers. Regardless of what your training manager does, you are 100 percent responsible for

your development and your career. You are responsible for the
hard work of assessing who you are, exploring what you want to
be, and creating a plan for your own development. By aggressively using the instructor tools in this book, you will live up to
that responsibility.

15

Ensuring the Success
of Instructors

---

*Instructors will perform with excellence if
they have the tools to perform the job.*

---

he purpose of this chapter is to review the instructor performance system, summarize the concepts presented in this book,
and show instructors and training managers how to use this
book as a tool to successfully implement these ideas.

The instructor performance system described in this
book is a tool designed to elicit excellent performance from
instructors. It is based on the premise that instructors will
perform with excellence if they are capable, have well-defined
jobs, know what is expected of them, receive feedback and
rewards that reinforce and develop excellent performance, and
have the tools to do the job.

Being capable is defined as possessing the skills, knowledge, experience, qualifications, and characteristics required to
do the instructor's job. The requirements of the instructor's job
are detailed in Chapter Two.

Chapter Three outlines the system that enables training
managers to select instructor candidates who possess these requirements. The three-part selection system enables training

managers to prepare for, conduct, and evaluate the results of a skill-based interview. It also provides data useful to developing capabilities in candidates selected to perform the instructor's job.

Instructors will perform with excellence if they have well-defined jobs. A good description of the instructor's job should define why the instructor position exists, specify areas of responsibility, and identify the skills, knowledge, qualifications, experience, and characteristics required and desired of excellent instructors.

Instructors also need to know what is expected of them. Performance expectations let instructors know what they are expected to do in their job. The instructor performance standards listed in Chapter Four and detailed in Chapters Five through Eleven clarify what is expected of all classroom instructors. These sixty performance standards define minimal levels of acceptable instructor performance in seven areas: preparation; participation; platform skills; content and sequencing; questioning techniques; use of training aids; and participant, course, and instructor evaluation. These standards are the ideal vehicle for clearly communicating what is expected of instructors. They also form the basis for providing instructor feedback and rewards.

The feedback system detailed in Chapter Twelve, the recognition and reward system described in Chapter Thirteen, and the development system detailed in Chapter Fourteen are all tools to reinforce excellent instructor performance and develop performance that can be improved. The feedback system includes two forms of feedback, motivational and developmental. Motivational feedback reinforces performance that meets and exceeds expectations. Developmental feedback strengthens and develops performance, including performance that falls short of expectations. While motivational feedback is akin to the concept of positive feedback, developmental feedback is more akin to the notion of coaching.

These forms of feedback can be used to provide ongoing, informal feedback as well as more formal feedback such as progress reviews and performance appraisals. The feedback tools presented in this book are simple and powerful. They will change forever the way you reinforce and develop excellent performance.

The feedback system provides key input into the recognition and reward systems. There is no limit to the number of ways training managers can recognize and reward instructors for excellent performance. However, most methods fall into two categories: formal and informal. The formal ways of recognizing and rewarding instructors include salary increases, bonuses, individual and team awards, prizes, promotions and other job moves, and opportunities for development. With the exception of development, most of the formal rewards are subject to rigid policy guidelines and as such cannot be administered with much flexibility. Development and the informal rewards aren't subject to such rigor. Consequently, these rewards are limited only by the training manager's creativity and resourcefulness. Chapter Thirteen lists ninety-nine ways to informally recognize and reward instructors.

An effective reward program reinforces desired instructor performance because it matches rewards to what instructors value, because it sends the right message, and because it is appropriate to the performance. An effective program also ensures that rewards are given sincerely and, when appropriate, privately rather than publicly.

Another tool for reinforcing instructor performance is development. There are two ways to look at development. One is from the standpoint of developing instructors to perform with excellence in the instructor's job; the other is from the standpoint of career development. Regardless of how you look at development, it should begin the day the newly selected instructor arrives on the job and end on the day the instructor leaves the organization.

By addressing development on day one, training managers are setting in place a process that will have an immediate and positive impact on instructor performance. The first day on the job is the perfect time for training managers to let newly selected instructors know what areas of skill they need to strengthen or develop and put together a plan to achieve that.

This instant attention to instructor development increases the likelihood that instructors will meet and exceed instructor performance standards and reduces the likelihood of classroom performance problems. By addressing development on day one, training managers will establish a reputation for being trustworthy and for helping instructors to do their job.

Each chapter in this book addresses development in one way or another. None however, speaks to development as specifically as Chapter Fourteen, which provides a host of tools that managers and instructors can use to focus attention on instructor development. Chapter Fourteen provides training managers with tools to develop all instructors, not just the fast-trackers or stars of the organization. Development takes many forms, including movement upward, sideways, and downward, as well as staying in place. Which form of development is appropriate for which instructor depends upon a combination of performance results and judgments of instructor potential.

Development for the high-performance, high-potential instructor is anything that leads upward, for example, a promotion, a key job assignment, an important special project, or a special educational program. Opportunities to update skills, experiences that enable instructors to keep abreast of training technology, attendance at professional conferences, and membership in professional organizations are all appropriate development activities for the high-performance, low-potential instructor. Appropriate skill training, a quick job move, or a change in supervision may be the right development step for the low-performance, high-potential instructor, while another chance, a downgrade, or outplacement are probably the best development activities for the low-performance, low-potential instructor. Time in the job, visible work assignments, exposure to decision makers, and periodic review of work are all appropriate development steps for instructors whose performance and/or potential is unknown.

The process of development is enhanced by agreement at higher levels of management and by involvement of the instructors. The development review is an ideal tool for reaching agreement among managers on instructor development. This agreement-based process extends responsibility for successful development to several levels of management and brings to light and addresses problems that generally are never addressed, such as how to attend to the development of instructors who are not moving up in an organization or how best to address differences in perceptions about an instructor's potential to move up.

Instructors must be involved in the development process if the process is to succeed at all. Instructors have a responsibility to seek out tools that enable them to know who they are, what they want to be, and how to get there. Unless the training manager has a clear idea of the aspirations of instructors, he or she is unlikely to act in ways that are perceived to be supportive. It's up to instructors to let their training managers know what they aspire to do. No one is better equipped than the instructor to do the hard work of self-assessment, exploration, and planning required to identify these aspirations.

Both instructors and training managers are responsible for development discussions, both the short-term, on-the-job kind of development discussion and the long-term, career type of development discussion. Training managers are responsible for identifying an instructor's aspirations, resolving any differences in perceptions of the instructor's performance and potential, reaching and documenting agreement on development steps, and following up, as appropriate. The instructor is responsible for being well prepared for these discussions, facing up to the realities of differing perceptions (if any), and taking action on the agreed development steps.

The preceding fourteen chapters contain all the tools instructors require to perform with excellence. Together, these tools form a powerful performance system that enables training managers to bring about excellence in instructor performance. Whether you are an instructor or a training manager, this book is your toolkit for excellent instructor performance.

The rest of this chapter is intended to help you successfully use these tools in your organization. First let's look at what training managers can do to successfully implement the instructor performance system, and then let's focus on what instructors can do to implement the ideas and concepts in this book.

Role of the Training Manager

As a training manager, you are in an ideal position to implement the instructor performance system. With the exception of the formal reward and recognition programs, which are rigidly ensconced in most organizations, choosing how to manage the remaining components of the instructor performance system is generally left to the training manager. Chapter Four suggests a way training managers can adapt the instructor performance standards to their own organization. You may recall that the key to successfully adapting the standards is to gain the agreement of key personnel, namely, your boss, peers, and subordinates. Agreement is the key, too, in successfully implementing the instructor performance system. When you cannot obtain this agreement, you can still successfully implement this system with instructors who report to you by adhering to the following six steps.

Step 1. Distribute copies of this book to your instructors and ask them to come prepared to discuss how you can successfully implement the instructor performance system described in this book.

Step 2. Review each section of the book and note areas where there is common agreement. Pay particular attention to the instructor performance standards and the step-by-step process for adapting these standards listed in Chapter Four. Set aside any disagreements until later.

Step 3. If you come across a concept or idea that does not apply to your organization, agree to eliminate it or adapt it to fit your organization.

Step 4. If the instructor performance system is missing components that are important or unique to your organization, simply add these to the system as appropriate.

Step 5. By now, you have reached agreement on the vast majority of concepts presented in this book. Now you must come to agreement on those areas where there was disagreement. Given the fact that until now all of your work on these steps has been based on agreement, it is likely that the areas of disagreement will be resolved easily and satisfactorily.

Step 6. Gain the commitment of participants to make the implementation of the instructor performance system successful, assign responsibility for implementing the system, and establish a realistic timetable for implementing the system and measuring and reviewing progress.

These steps are the key to successful implementation of the instructor performance system. Once you have completed them, you will be well on your way to achieving trainer excellence.

Role of the Instructor

If you are an instructor, you have a number of choices to make relative to implementing the concepts presented in this book. You can choose to gain the support of your boss and/or your peers to implement the instructor performance system, or you can go it alone and implement only those components of the system that you can directly control. Let's look at each of these choices.

If you suspect your boss might welcome the concepts presented here and you are willing to do whatever needs to be done to help implement such a system, then you might begin by preparing a presentation (following the outline of this book) that describes the instructor performance system and its benefits. If your boss expresses interest in pursuing the opportunity after you make your presentation, give him or her a copy of this book and offer to do whatever you can to help make it easy for your boss to pursue implementation of the instructor performance system. This might include making a similar presentation to your peers or to higher management. It might include contacting other organizations that employ such a system or exploring consultants who offer professional assistance in this area. At some point, your boss will need to follow the steps listed above that describe what training managers can do to successfully implement an instructor performance system.

If your boss is not someone you are willing to consult, consider following the same steps with other instructors in your organization. By enrolling their support to implement the ideas presented here, you may find a way to gain your boss's support for implementation of the entire system.

If you choose neither of the above options and decide to go it alone, there is much you can do to progress toward excellence. Each of the tools presented in this book was designed so that you can make good use of them with little adaptation. For example, you can use or adapt the instructor job definition in Chapter Two. You can use the instructor performance standards listed in Chapter Four and detailed in Chapters Five through Eleven, or you can adapt them for your own use by following the guidelines presented in Chapter Four. You can gain valuable feedback by using the instructor assessment tool in Chapter Twelve. You can influence progress reviews and performance appraisals by taking care to document your performance results and make this documentation available to your training manager. Remember the story of Bob in Chapter Thirteen? You, too, can influence the recognition and rewards you receive by following a similar path, and you can affect your own career development by following the steps outlined in Chapter Fourteen.

How to Avoid Failure

The tools presented in this book make it possible to achieve excellence; however, there are three common reasons these efforts can fail. Let's look at them.

First of all, the effort is doomed to failure if training managers don't take the time to gain the agreement and participation of instructors to adapt and implement the instructor performance system. This is not always an easy process. Experienced instructors sometimes react negatively to any system with standards or guidelines for instruction. Their rationale is that because they have been instructing for a long time, such standards are obvious. Of course they are obvious; that is one of the benefits of having standards. They let instructors know what is obviously expected of them. However, a new instructor may not know what is obvious unless there are performance standards. By giving both new and experienced instructors the opportunity to participate in the implementation of the instructor performance system, you increase the likelihood that the implementation will be successful. Anytime people feel something is being shoved down their throats, they resist. If instructors feel that is what is happening with the instructor performance system, they will resist until the effort fails. It is essential to include them in the implementation.

Secondly, the effort is doomed to failure if you are not extremely cautious about what components of the system you eliminate. For example, it may be suggested that you eliminate job descriptions from the system because you already have job descriptions in your organization. However, unless those job descriptions contain a complete listing of required responsibilities, skills, knowledge, experience, qualifications, and characteristics, as detailed in Chapter Two, they are useless for managing performance. Each component of the instructor performance system links to, and as a result affects, every other component of the system. For example, job descriptions are the basis for selecting instructors and establishing performance standards. If you tamper with the job description, you may need to alter the selection system and the instructor performance standards, as well as other components of the system. By eliminating any part of the system, you run the risk of destroying the entire system. So be cautious in what you eliminate.

Thirdly, no matter how carefully you introduce the instructor performance system, it is doomed to failure if you do not review progress toward the successful implementation of the system. Progress reviews with instructors are essential to successful implementation. Most new systems fail because the only contact employees ever have with them is when they are introduced. In other words, once the system was implemented, that was the last anyone ever heard of it. If you want the instructor performance system to be successful you have got to pay the same kind of attention to monitoring its successful implementation as you did to its introduction.

If you are a training manager, the tools you have reviewed in this chapter will enable you to carefully implement a system that will achieve instructor excellence. If you are an instructor, these tools will enable you to develop into an excellent instructor and take charge of your career in a way you never dreamed possible.

In Chapter One, I said that this book is about bringing instructor excellence to life. Frankly, excellence is a rare commodity in today's workplace. Yet when it does exist, one can always sense it—there's a passion for quality and a spark of excitement in the air. The excellent organization appears to hum along like a piece of finely crafted machinery; people feel purposeful and valued and come to realize that it is possible to be a human being in the workplace and produce excellence at the same time. These are feelings that, once experienced, are never forgotten.

The instructor performance system is not an instant cure-all for poor performance or a miracle that will cause excellence overnight. However, a carefully implemented, well-executed instructor performance system will result in excellent performance by instructors.

APPENDIX:

Typical Classroom Problems

Excessive Talking Among Participants

Step 1. Decide if the talking is OK or disruptive. If it's OK, ignore it.

Step 2. If it's disruptive, do the following until the behavior stops:

- Attempt to involve participants.
- Pause, be silent for a few seconds, and see if letting participants hear themselves quiets them.
- Move closer to the people talking (do not go right up to them).
- Refer back to something one of them may have said earlier (acknowledge participants).

Step 3. If the behavior persists, stay calm, nondefensive, and nonthreatening and do the following:

- Temporarily rearrange seating (go into an exercise requiring people to work in pairs and separate talkative participants).
- Permanently rearrange seating (leave talkative participants in new seats, apart from one another).

Step 4. If talking still exists, take these final actions as necessary:

- Call a break and talk to participants privately.
- Tell participants that you are anxious to have them partici-pate and that their talking is disruptive to what you are trying to accomplish.
- Ask participants if they are willing to refrain from talking to one another.
- Explain the consequences of continuing to talk (removal from class).
- Dismiss participants from classroom.

If at any step along the way the participants cease the disruptive behavior, take the opportunity to reinforce their new behavior. For example, if they have stopped talking and started to participate, you can say (privately), "Thanks for participating, it's good to have your input."

The above steps, or some variation of them, are appropri-ate for many different classroom disruptions, including making wisecracks and making noise.

Participant Challenges Instructor

Participants who sharply or aggressively challenge an instructor usually pose a dilemma. Do you (the instructor) take advantage of the power of your position and put the challenger down, or do you find ways to handle the challenge that are mutually produc-tive? While you may be inclined to the former, that action will increase the likelihood of a classroom disaster and greatly re-duce the likelihood that participants will meet training objec-tives. By choosing to handle the challenge productively, you increase the likelihood of creating an exhilarating learning experience for participants. At the same time, you will develop a high level of skill in this difficult area.

The response to this kind of situation draws on some of the concepts of transactional analysis discussed in Chapter One and on performance standard 45 (see Chapter Nine), which addresses the issue of being nondefensive. You might refer to these two chapters as you review the following steps.

Step 1. Decide if the challenge is productive or unproductive.

Step 2. If it is productive, continue the dialogue; if it's unproductive, determine the level of tension the challenge has created in the room.

Step 3. If the tension in the room is extremely high, consider taking a break and talking to the challenger in private.

Step 4. If the tension is within reason, respond from either your adult state or your creative child state to reduce or break the tension.

Step 5. Once the tension is reduced or broken, begin to get at the specifics of the challenge. In other words, find out what is really troubling the challenger. Use open-ended questions: "Why do you feel so strongly about this?" "What specifically troubles you about this?"

Step 6. Once the specifics of the challenge are out in the open, respond appropriately. Thank the challenger and state what (if any) action you are willing to take to respond to the situation.

These are difficult situations to handle. It will help if you avoid sugarcoated responses or defensive behavior and acknowledge any mistakes you may have made in handling the situation.

Participant Asks Irrelevant Questions

This situation is a simple one to handle. A wonderful ground rule to use is: if it takes longer to tell the person the question is irrelevant than it does to answer the question, then just answer the question. (Performance standard 48 in Chapter Nine also addresses this situation.) Use the following steps to handle irrelevant questions.

Step 1. If the answer is short, use the ground rule given above. In other words, answer the question if someone asks, "Where did you get your briefcase?"

Step 2. Look to tie the question to the subject matter at

hand. For example, suppose the subject is decision making and someone says, "Where did you get your briefcase?" Answer the question and follow up with something like, "What decision-making processes do you use when purchasing a briefcase?"

Step 3. If the number of irrelevant questions becomes disruptive, privately ask the person to hold off asking such questions until break or after hours, when you will answer any questions you can.

Step 4. If the behavior continues, privately explain that the behavior is disruptive and ask if the person is willing to stop asking so many questions. If the answer is yes, thank the person. If the answer is no, explain the consequences of continuing to ask irrelevant questions. If the behavior continues, carry out the consequences stated.

People who ask irrelevant questions are generally looking for some kind of acknowledgment. Consequently, this behavior can often be stopped altogether or controlled easily by giving the participant some positive reinforcement.

Nonparticipation

There are many reasons why people do not participate in training classes. The person may be reluctant because of previous unpleasant experiences in the classroom. It may be that the person was forced to attend the training program, or has a million and one other things to do, or is shy in public. Regardless of the reasons why some people do not participate, the following steps should garner adequate participation.

Step 1. Involve the nonparticipant by doing any or all of the following:

- Use open-ended questions.
- Use positive reinforcement techniques; for example, refer to something the nonparticipant said earlier or a subject in which the nonparticipant is known to be an expert.
- Use the nonparticipant's name frequently.
- When speaking, move close to the nonparticipant.

- Establish and maintain good eye contact with the non-participant.
- Throw questions to areas of the room that include the nonparticipant; for example, "What ideas do you in the back of the room have?"
- Use safe but pointed questions such as "Sue, you have substantial experience in this area; how would you handle this?" Follow up such questions with positive recognition or reinforcement, such as "Thanks, Sue, for your comments."

Step 2. Talk to the person at break; mention that you look forward to hearing his or her thoughts in the classroom. Ask if there is anything you can do that would make it comfortable for the person to participate.

Step 3. If none of the actions taken above elicit participation, talk to the nonparticipant privately. Tell the nonparticipant that you expect each trainee to participate and ask the person to participate. If the person refuses, explain the consequences, if any, and ask again for participation.

Step 4. If the person participates, provide positive reinforcement. If the person remains a nonparticipant, take appropriate measures.

Arriving Late or Leaving Early

Participants who arrive late or leave early often disrupt training. Many instructors make the mistake of waiting for latecomers. In effect, such behavior rewards the latecomers and punishes the participants who have arrived on time, which in turn gives unspoken permission to all participants to be late. The following steps will help you handle this problem.

Step 1. Start class on time at the beginning and after all breaks, including lunch.

Step 2. At the beginning of class ask participants to tell you if they know that there is any portion of the program they will miss.

Step 3. Let participants know that you will commit to ending on time if they are willing to be on time at the start of the day and after each break, including lunch. Ask directly if that's something they are willing to do.

Step 4. Thank participants who show up on time and ignore those who are late the first time.

Step 5. If a participant is developing a pattern of being late, meet privately with the person, point out the behavior, and ask what the person will do to be on time. If necessary, make sure the person understands the consequences if the problem continues.

Step 6. At the start of the next class segment, provide positive reinforcement if the person comes in on time and take appropriate measures if the person comes in late.

Equipment Failures

Most of the problems associated with equipment failure can be prevented if certain actions are taken in advance. The following steps are intended to enable you to effectively prepare for an equipment failure.

Step 1. Have a practice run just before class begins. A practice run will tell you whether your equipment is operative.

Step 2. Secure a set of spare projector bulbs and parts, as appropriate, and learn how to install them. By having spares at your disposal, you will avoid the problems associated with bulbs burning out and parts breaking down.

Step 3. Have a list (with phone numbers) of technicians or contacts who can be called upon in the event of a power outage or equipment breakdown.

Step 4. Develop a set of alternative plans for the class in the event of an equipment failure.

These simple prevention steps will enable you to effectively handle equipment failures that crop up from time to time. On those occasions when you are not prepared, don't panic—there is often someone available who knows exactly what to do. When these things happen, smile and do whatever you need to do to meet the objectives set out in the training program.

REFERENCES

"Bob Powers: An Unconventional Success Story." *Training: The Magazine of Human Resource Development*, Aug. 1986, pp. 65–66.

Feuer, D., and Geber, B. "Uh-Oh...Second Thoughts About Adult Learning Theory." *Training: The Magazine of Human Resource Development*, Dec. 1988, pp. 31–39.

Harris, T. A. *I'm OK, You're OK: A Practical Guide to Transactional Analysis.* New York: Harper & Row, 1969.

Mager, R. F. *Making Instruction Work.* Belmont, Calif.: Lake Books, 1988.

Nadler, L., and Nadler, Z. *Developing Human Resources.* (3rd ed.) San Francisco: Jossey-Bass, 1989.

Tosti, D. T. *Introduction to Performance Technology.* Washington, D.C.: National Society for Performance and Instruction, 1986.

"Training Magazine's Industry Report 1990." *Training: The Magazine of Human Resource Development*, Oct. 1990, pp. 29–32.

INDEX

193–196; privacy issues and, 192–193; reaching agreement concerning, 189–191; responsibility for, 183–184; steps for effective, 196–201; training programs for, 201–202

Instructor Development Plan, 193, 194

Instructor evaluation: and instructor performance system, 9; of self, 143–144. *See also* Feedback

Instructor Interview Form, 38–41

Instructor performance: annual appraisal of, 165–170; assessment tool for observation of, 156–157; components of, 8–10; difficulties in, 161–164; expectations regarding, 9, 207; observation of, 154–155, 158; progress review of, 158–159; review of previous, 65–66

Instructor Performance Appraisal Form, 165–168

Instructor performance system: instructor evaluation and, 9; job definition and, 9, 11–12; purpose of, 206; rewards and, 9–10, 208

Instructor Preparation Checklist, 58, 59

Instructor Progress Review Form, 158–160

Instructor selection: analyzing pre-interview data for, 26–28; announcing open position for, 25–26; basis of good, 24–25; concluding activities following, 45–46; importance of, 23–24; interviewing and, 27, 29–40, 41–45

Instructor Selection Form, 26–28, 45

Instructors: accessibility of, 68–70; answers provided by, 115–118; challenges to, 69–70, 218–219; defining one's role as, 19–22; determining what is valued by, 172–173; need for, 13–14;

performance and potential ratings for, 184–185 (*see also* Instructor performance); responsibilities of, 14–15, 212–213; role in self-development, 202–205; skills required of, 15–19, 29–38

Interpersonal skills assessment, 29–30

Interviews: activities following, 45–46; analysis of pre-interview data for, 26–28; assessment of candidate during, 27, 29–40; importance of preparation for, 27; steps in conducting skill-based, 39, 41–45

Irrelevant questions, 120–121, 219–220. *See also* Questions

J

Job announcements, for instructor positions, 25–26

Job definition: characteristics of, 12–13; example of instructor, 20–21; and instructor performance system, 9, 11–12

Job tools, and instructor performance system, 9

K

Knowledge: questions to test for, 113–115; requirements regarding, 15–17

Knowles, Malcolm, 5

L

Language, use of biased, 78–80
Leadership skills assessment, 30
Learning ability, 5
Lighting, classroom, 61

M

Maintenance of training aids, 131
Management by objectives, 48
Management skills assessment, 37